the BEGINNER'S GUIDE

the Internet

Everything you need to learn and use the Internet

OUR MISSION

In most computer applications, students, supervisors, employees and users seldom use all the features available in their software. What most people need is the knowledge to do or perform specific tasks, quickly and easily. They need the ability to painlessly learn how to write a letter, report, budget or set up a mailing list. The Beginner's Guide uses everyday examples to guide readers step-by-step through the commands they will use the most to perform these tasks. Clear, understandable lessons combined with concise illustrations provide the information you need to learn and understand most software and features used in everyday tasks.

INST Publishing is committed to providing proven solutions for both corporations and individuals to easily and quickly learn their computer software. Established in 1989, INST Publishing offers high quality software training products that reflect the company's unique understanding of the new ways in which individuals and businesses must work together to achieve success. INST's innovative approach is evident in a class of training guides that allows information to be accessed and communicated in easy to understand terms.

by

A trademark of Instant Information Inc.

A WIZARDWORKS Company
3850 Annapolis Lane, Minneapolis, MN 55447

Printed in the U.S.A.

Joseph Garcia

The BEGINNER'S GUIDE for INTERNET
Published by: INST Publishing, a division of Instant Information Inc.

ISBN 1-881023-95-8

Printed in the United States of America.

Cover Design by
Shaun Wolden Design

Acknowledgments
Special thanks to the dedicated staff at INST Publishing

Table of Contents

Table of Contents

Your Personal Computer

1 When setting up your system, location is very important. Your computer must have room for proper air circulation so that your CPU and Monitor don't over heat. Don't put the computer in an enclosed cabinet or close against a wall.

Once your computer is set up, never unplug an interface cable or the power cord while the computer is running. You could lose important data or damage your computer components. You should also protect your PC from power fluctuations by plugging all power cords into a surge protector.

2 Your PC is made up of a collection of various components that interact together as one unit. The essential parts of your PC are:

CPU (Central Processing Unit)
Monitor
Keyboard
Mouse
Printer

3 Disk drives are used to store software programs and data files. The three types of disk drives are floppy disk drives, hard disk drives and CD-ROM disk drives. Floppy disk drives store data on removable diskettes that are either 5 1/4" or 3 1/2" in diameter. Hard disk drives are usually mounted inside the PC. CD-ROM disk drives are a read-only disk drive designed to access and read the data encoded on compact disks and to transfer this data to a computer.

Because of the hard plastic casing, the smaller 3 1/2 inch disk is able to store more data than the older 5 1/4 inch disk. A CD-ROM disk can store vast amounts of information because it uses light to record data in a form that's more tightly packed than the 3 1/2 inch disk. However, like a music CD, a computer CD is a read-only device; you can't use it to store your own data.

4 Software programs send instructions to different parts of the computer through a special set of programs called an operating system. The operating system's programs are responsible for starting up the computer, loading programs and controlling the PC's keyboard, monitor, printer, serial and parallel port and disk drives. DOS is usually pre-installed on your hard disk by the manufacturer.

5 The start-up cycle when you turn on your PC is called booting your system. During the boot(start-up) process, your PC will load portions of DOS into its Random Access Memory. Computers use Random Access Memory, or RAM, to process software programs. The initial boot process is called a "cold" boot. You can also restart your PC after it has been turned on by performing a "warm" boot. To perform a warm boot, press **CTRL+ALT+DEL** together.

Your Personal Computer

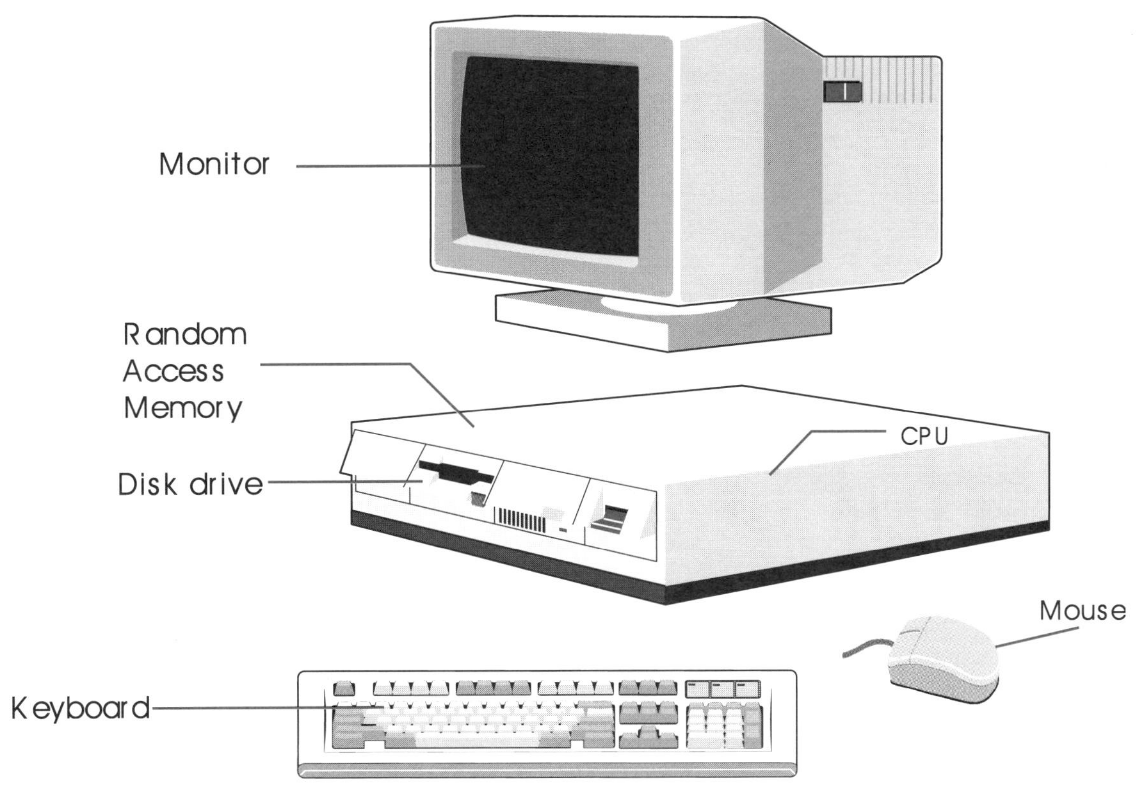
Monitor
Random Access Memory
CPU
Disk drive
Mouse
Keyboard

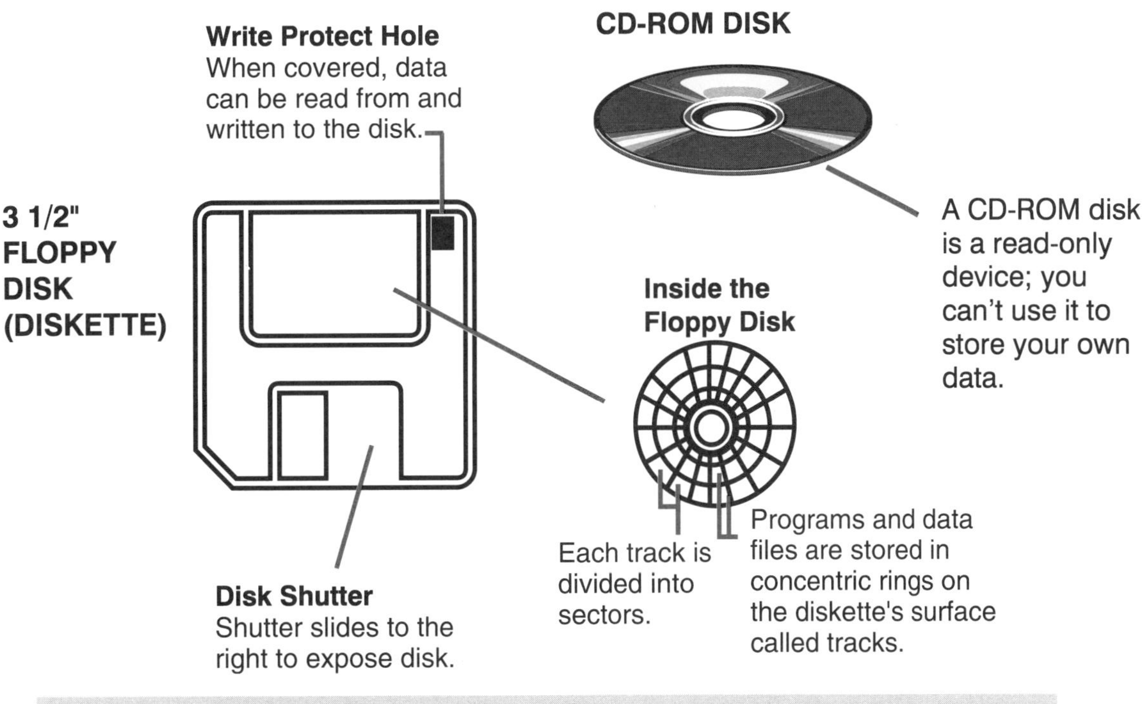
Write Protect Hole
When covered, data can be read from and written to the disk.
CD-ROM DISK
3 1/2" FLOPPY DISK (DISKETTE)
A CD-ROM disk is a read-only device; you can't use it to store your own data.
Inside the Floppy Disk
Programs and data files are stored in concentric rings on the diskette's surface called tracks.
Each track is divided into sectors.
Disk Shutter
Shutter slides to the right to expose disk.

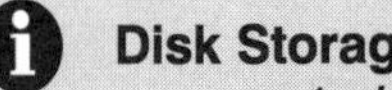

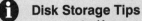

Disk Storage Tips

1. *Keep magnets away from floppies and hard disks.*
2. *Keep telephones away from floppies.*

Your Personal Computer

1 Random Access Memory (RAM) is the computer's primary working memory in which program instructions and data are stored so that they are accessible directly to the CPU. It is important to remember that RAM only works when the computer is turned off.

2 The Motherboard is the main circuit board in your PC where all other components are mounted.

3 The CPU, which is short for Central Processing Unit, is your PC's most important component. It does all your PC's thinking and runs all your programs.

4 The Power Supply provides all the computer components with the correct power voltages. The power supply converts your High-Voltage current into the required low voltage current.

5 Read Only Memory (ROM) has permanent data written on the ROM chip during manufacturing. This data is always there, even when your PC is turned off.

6 The Video Card takes all the stored memory images generated by your PC and links them to the monitor for display.

7 The Disk Drive Controller Card controls your PC's disk drives and transfers data.

8 The Battery, which most people are surprised to learn that their computer has, powers a clock that keeps track of time when the computer is turned off. It also maintains low voltage electricity to certain RAM chips that have a record of what components are installed in your system.

9 Ports are entry/exit boundary mechanisms that govern and synchronize the flow of data into and out of the CPU from and to external devices such as printers and modems.

10 The Floppy Disk Drive consists of a slot to accept a floppy disk, a motor that spins the disk and a recording/reading device that moves across the disk in order to read or write data.

11 The Hard Disk Drive is the main permanent storage unit, holding large amounts of data and programs. The data on your hard drive is not affected when you turn off the PC. It remains there unless you overwrite it or the hard disk is damaged.

Your PC is best left undisturbed, but if you must open the case, remember to disconnect your PC from the power source.

Your Personal Computer

This typical cross section of a computer will give you an idea of what you are looking at when you remove the cover.

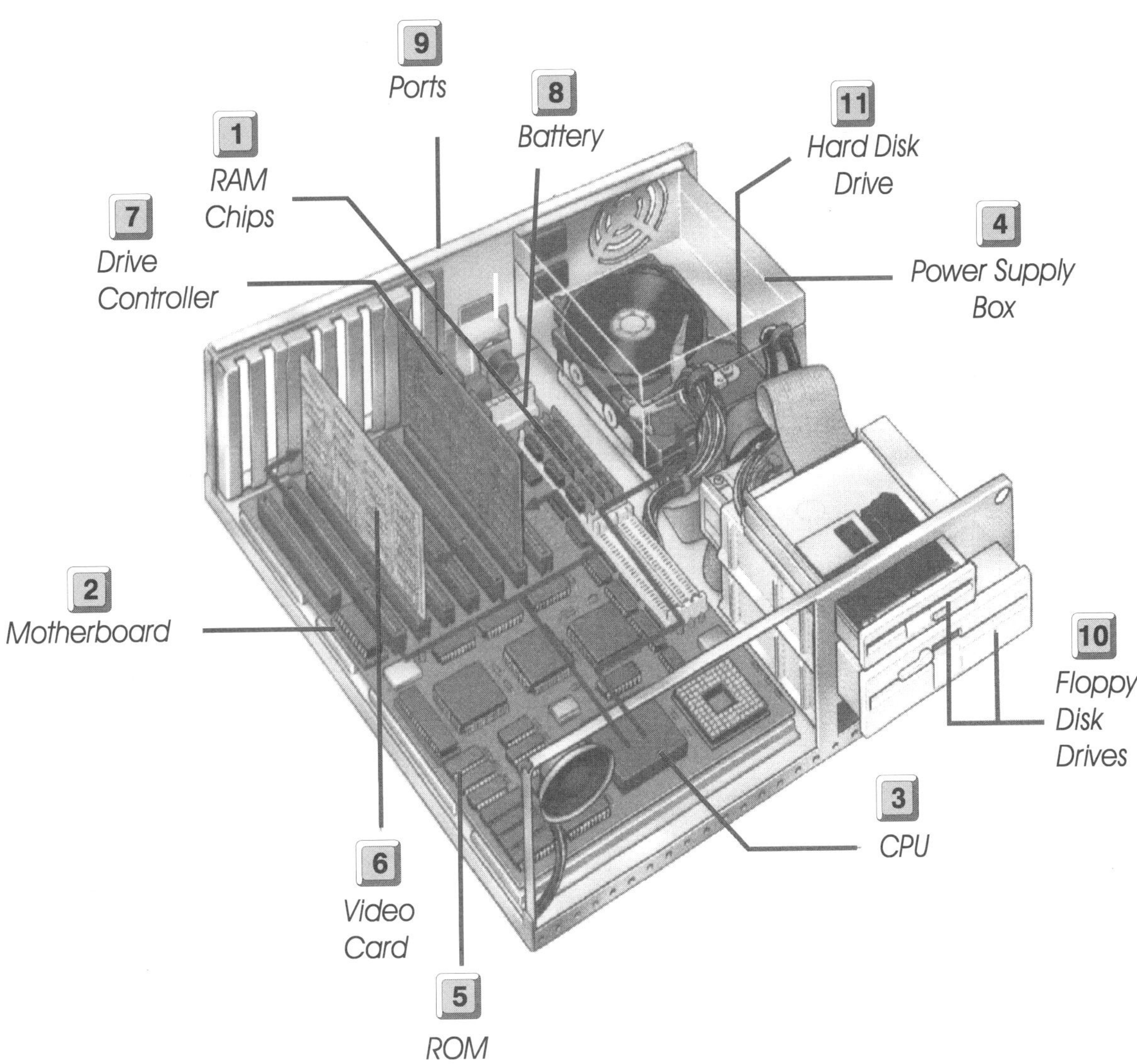

Always be sure the power is disconnected before removing the computer cover or any of it's components.

Connecting with NetCruiser

SYSTEM REQUIREMENTS

To operate NetCruiser for Windows you will need at least a 386 IBM PC-compatible system running MS-DOS 5.0 or greater and Windows 3.1 or greater. You should have at least 4 megabytes of RAM and at least 4 megabytes of free hard disk space. Make sure all of the fonts that install with Windows are in the Windows control panel, true type fonts are enabled and the "Show only true type fonts" is not checked. You will also need a 9600 Baud or faster modem.

INSTALLING NETCRUISER

1. Insert the disk into drive a: or b:.
2. From the Program Manager choose File, Run.
3. Enter a:setup or b:setup (which ever one applies) in the Run dialog box.
4. Choose a modem type, baud rate, and COM port in the dialog presented
5. Select a NETCOM telephone number that is near your location. After installation you will have a new program group called "NETCOM" which contains NetCruiser, NetCruiser Help, NetCruiser Registration, NetCruiser Getting Started Help, and the NetCruiser upgrade program.

REGISTERING WITH NETCRUISER

You will need to have a credit card ready in order to complete the following steps:

1. From the NETCOM program group in Program Manager, click the NetCruiser Registration icon.
2. Click **OK** in the "Welcome to NetCruiser" dialog box. Fill in the "Registration Information" form. If a Registration code is printed on your disk label, be sure to enter the code when prompted. If there isn't a code, click **Continue** on the Registration Code dialog box.
3. Fill in the appropriate boxes for your modem to reach the NETCOM toll-free registration number. Then click **OK**.
4. Fill in your credit card information.
5. Make sure your modem is set for hardware (RTS/CTS) flow control. To check this, go to the Windows control panel, select **Ports**, then highlight the port that is connected to your modem. Click on **Settings**, go to the last item in the list and change Flow control to Hardware.

CONNECTING WITH NETCRUISER

1. From the NETCOM program group select NetCruiser.
2. NetCruiser will display status messages across the dialog box in the center of your display. When the connection is made, choose Help from the menu bar for help in using NetCruiser. Review newsgroups for postings with your questions. Look in the Netcom.NetCruiser.General and Netcom.NetCruiser.Tech newsgroups for a good source of information. Most of the time the answer to your question has already been posted so it is best to spend some time reading the newsgroups before making a post.

If you need immediate help, you can reach NETCOM customer support at 408-983-5970. If you don't need an immediate response, you can E-Mail customer support at SUPPORT@IX.NETCOM.COM.

Assumptions

INST Publishing Beginner's Guides are designed to help business people master the leading software programs as quickly as possible. By working through the lessons in this guide you will be able to use the Internet with NetCruiser in the shortest possible time.

ASSUMPTIONS

This Beginner's Guide assumes you have installed NetCruiser on your hard disk using the complete setup option in the directory suggested by NETCOM.

This guide also assumes that you are familiar with Microsoft Windows or Windows for Workgroups, and that you are using a Microsoft Windows compatible mouse, trackball or other pointing device.

This is not a typing tutorial. Data entry has been kept to a minimum so that you can focus on learning the Internet and NetCruiser as quickly as possible.

Most of the lessons in this guide require an Internet connection with NetCruiser.

CONVENTIONS

NetCruiser allows you to enter some commands using the mouse or the keyboard.

When you are asked to select menu options, the options will be displayed in bold type, such as **File**, **Close**.

When it is time to press a key or select a button, the name of the key or button will appear in bold type. For example, "Press **Enter**" means to press the key marked **Enter** on you keyboard. "Click **OK**" means to use the mouse to click on the **OK** button, or press the **Tab** key until the button is outlined and then press **Enter**.

To perform some tasks you may need to press two keys simultaneously. If you are asked to press **Ctrl+F10**, hold down the Ctrl key and while you hold it down, press the **F10** key, then release both keys. Keys that are separated by commas, such as "**Alt**, **F**, **O**" should be pressed sequentially.

Information boxes provide helpful tips and advanced information.

How to Use this Book

Guaranteed the Fastest and Easiest way to learn new software

This book is designed to help you become software proficient in the shortest possible time. Each turned page represents a complete lesson, written in easy to understand, non-technical terms. Each lesson includes step-by-step instructions, practical examples and clear illustrations. The step-by-step instructions avoid computer jargon and lead the reader from simple tasks to advanced techniques. The examples and illustrations are based on practical "real world" tasks performed by most users.

How The BEGINNER'S GUIDE is organized

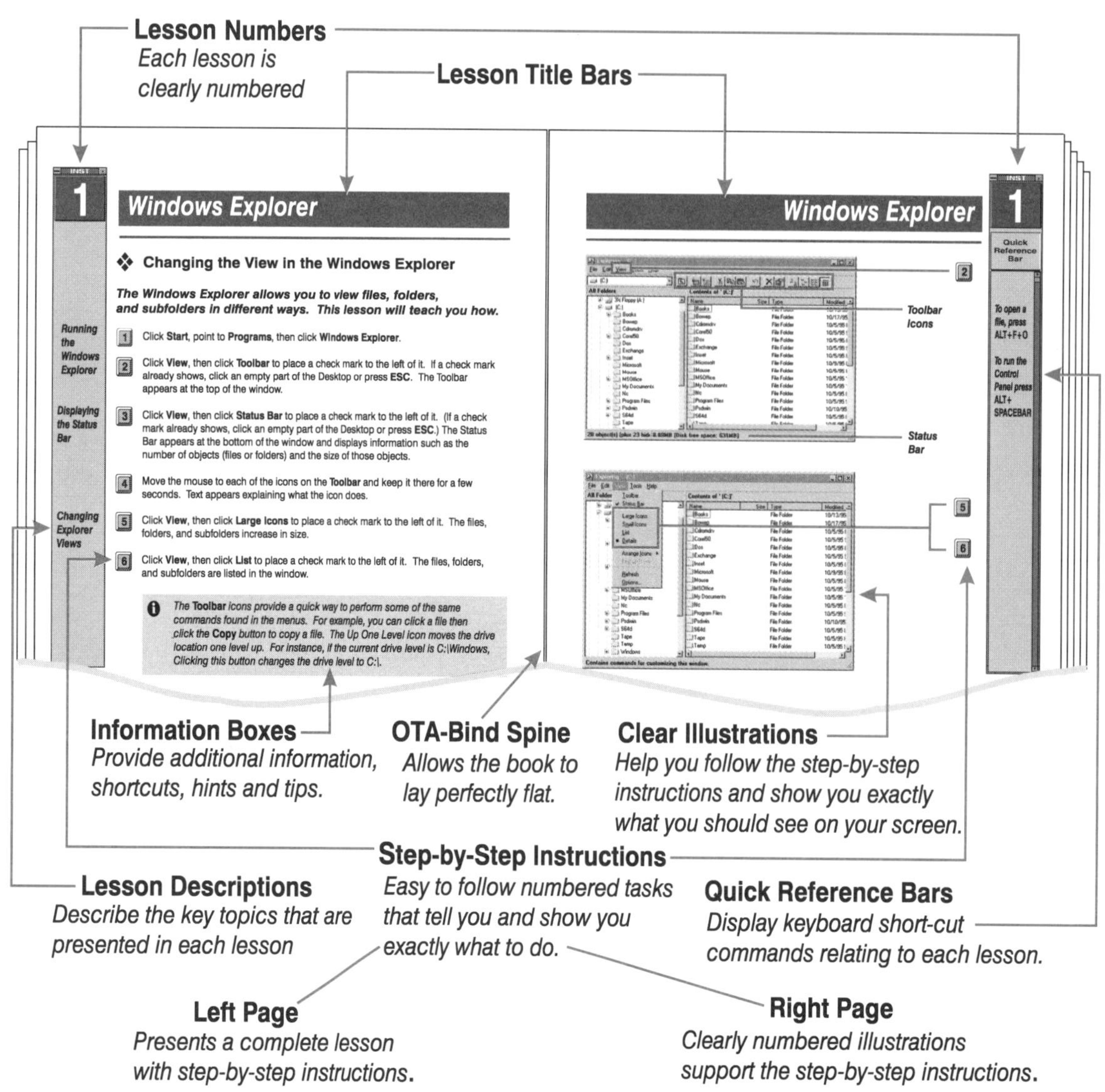

Lesson Numbers
Each lesson is clearly numbered
Lesson Title Bars
Windows Explorer
Changing the View in the Windows Explorer
Windows Explorer
Quick Reference Bar
Toolbar Icons
Status Bar
Information Boxes
Provide additional information, shortcuts, hints and tips.
OTA-Bind Spine
Allows the book to lay perfectly flat.
Clear Illustrations
Help you follow the step-by-step instructions and show you exactly what you should see on your screen.
Step-by-Step Instructions
Easy to follow numbered tasks that tell you and show you exactly what to do.
Lesson Descriptions
Describe the key topics that are presented in each lesson
Quick Reference Bars
Display keyboard short-cut commands relating to each lesson.
Left Page
Presents a complete lesson with step-by-step instructions.
Right Page
Clearly numbered illustrations support the step-by-step instructions.

Working with the INTERNET

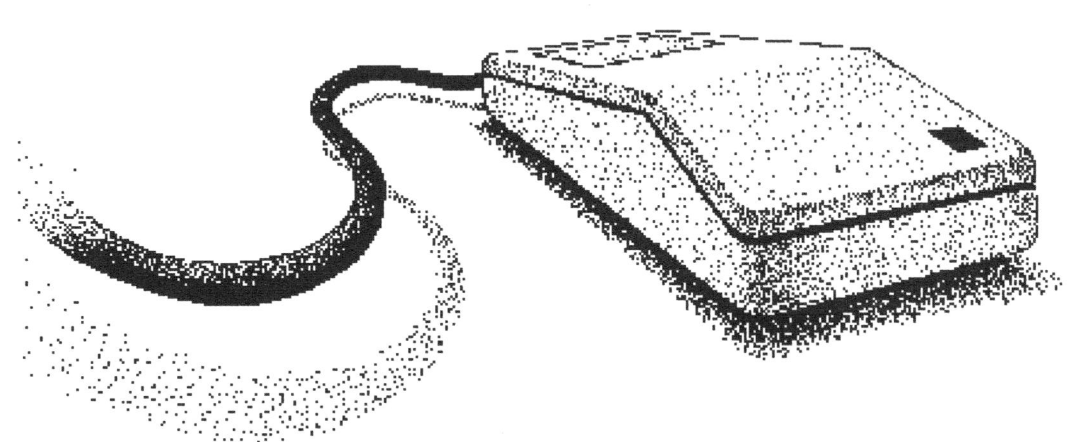

Overview of the Internet

The concept of the Internet was created in the 1960s by the Department of Defense. ARPANET (Advanced Research Projects Administration), was the first stage of today's "Superhighway" and was designed to be a loosely knit, highly decentralized group of networks without central authority or control. ARPANET served both as an experiment in reliable networking and linked the DOD with military research contractors, including universities doing military funded research. Reliable networking proved effective by using a scheme called dynamic rerouting. This scheme involved automatically rerouting traffic that had been disrupted, by using any alternate link that was available.

Based on its versatility and reliability ARPANET became very successful. Universities clambered to sign up and as the volume of users increased, the Net began to get more and more difficult to manage or control. To create some semblance of order, the military decided to divide the Net into two separate entities. MILNET which would contain the military sites and ARPANET which was designated to contain all the non-military sites. Although separate by design, both Milnet and Arpanet remained connected via a technical development called IP (Internet Protocol). All the designated networks connected by this process in the Internet speak IP and each can send and receive messages from one to the other. IP was also designed to accommodate thousands of networks and because of the design of the IP scheme, every computer on the IP network is just as capable as any other and can communicate with any other type of machine. This IP scheme means your home computer can be just as "powerful" as the largest mainframe. As a result, activity on ARPANET began to increase and at times the net was actually swamped by new workstations generating too much network traffic.

In 1982, the National Science Foundation created NSFNET which offered a high-speed communications network designed to permit widespread access by researchers and scientists to five super-computer centers spread across the country. NSFNET proved to be far more successful than anticipated and by the 1990's so much traffic had moved from ARPANET that it was no longer viable and was eventually shutdown. However, over time the supercomputers either didn't work or proved to be too expensive to operate and most customers found themselves using high-performance workstations instead. During this transition period, several large commercial networks had begun to emerge within the Internet and the true commercial Internet as we know it today was gaining more and more momentum. Fueled by companies such as IBM, Sprint, Microsoft and Alternet, the Internet has rapidly become the business tool of tomorrow.

From its origins of being the exclusive tool of the military and research scientists, the Internet now offers almost unlimited information to anyone who has a computer and a modem. You may enter the Internet world to discuss politics, check mortgage rates, plan a vacation or just catch up on today's news. Although still rough and ready in its new found popularity, the Internet offers the willing traveler excitement and adventure from their office or home.

Access to the Internet

NETCOM is a national Internet that provides physical access to the Internet. **NetCruiser** is software that allows you to connect to the world of the Internet. With **NetCruiser** you:

- May make a direct connection to the Internet and be a part of the Net.
- Have a "user friendly" interface which is easy to read and comprehend.
- Have all the tools necessary to explore the resources that lurk within the Internet.

Although **NetCruiser** gives you a direct connection to the Internet, you will establish your own address and the files you download are sent directly to your computer. You make this direct connection using a modem and the technical term for this is **SLIP**, short for Serial-Line Internet Protocol. **NetCruiser** is the first product to make **SLIP** accessible and easy to use. NETCOM is also one of only a handful of providers that makes direct connection to the Internet affordable.

NetCruiser's graphical interface and full-screen orientation means you can use your mouse in the familiar Window's format instead of using your keyboard. **NetCruiser** also allows you to use fast modems (currently, up to 38.4kb per second). Using data compression you can actually transfer certain kinds of data at a multiple of this speed. When you connect directly to the Internet, the faster the modem the better the performance.

Also upgrading is easy with **NetCruiser**. By choosing **D**ownload **N**ew **V**ersion from the File menu on **NetCruiser**, you may download the latest version or upgrade free.

NetCruiser software gives you Windows versions of the most important set of tools on the Internet.

- ***Mail***
- ***Usenet news***
- ***Telnet***
- ***FTP***
- ***Gopher***
- ***A World Wide Web graphical browser***.

Netcom has combined these tools in a way that simplifies the access to them all, makes them easy to use and you can use them together at the same time.

Getting Started

Email Guidelines

In this lesson you will learn the process of Electronic Mail and some general guidelines to follow when using Email.

Probably the service used most often on the Internet, Electronic Mail provides the exchange of messages between you and other Internet users anywhere in the world. Electronic Mail, or Email, uses Internet addresses for delivery to the recipient's Host computer (the remote computer used for storage and access, usually provided by an Internet Service Provider). Once at the Host, the message is available for retrieval from a Client (local) mail program like the one included with NetCruiser. If the address is wrong or not accessible for some reason a message is returned stating so.

Email Guidelines

Here are some general guidelines to follow when using Email:

1. **Be specific in the Subject line.** Use as clear a subject as you can. Recipients can then prioritize their messages. Plus, saved messages will have a quick reference of their contents.

2. **Be brief.** Say enough to deliver your objective then stop. Do not overload your message with needless detail. Remember that the reader will probably have numerous messages to keep up with each day.

3. **Include a salutation.** This is especially important for business correspondence. Avoiding this is similar to bombarding a co-worker with questions before the typical "Good morning. How are you..."

4. **Identify yourself.** Do not assume that the recipient will know who you are or will figure this out from the message header. If in doubt, include your name at the beginning of the message.

5. **Do not assume that your Email is private.** Unlike postal mail there is no guarantee your Email will not be read by unintended recipients.

6. **Use white space.** Break up your message into paragraphs when appropriate. Email with continuous text and no white space is intimidating to read.

7. **When replying to a message, include the pertinent content of the original message.** A reply with a simple "yes" or "no" answer may be confusing if the original sender forgets the question.

8. **Write in the active voice.** This style is always easier to read.

9. **Use proper English.** Messages should have correct spelling, punctuation and be grammatically correct.

10. **Read your message carefully before sending.** Make sure the message delivers its intended purpose. If the message is construed as negative or you were in a poor mood when it was written, you may want to wait a day or so and reread and change the message before sending.

Getting Started

Quick Reference Bar

Include a clear subject

Include a salutation

Identify yourself

Use white space

Include pertinent content in replies

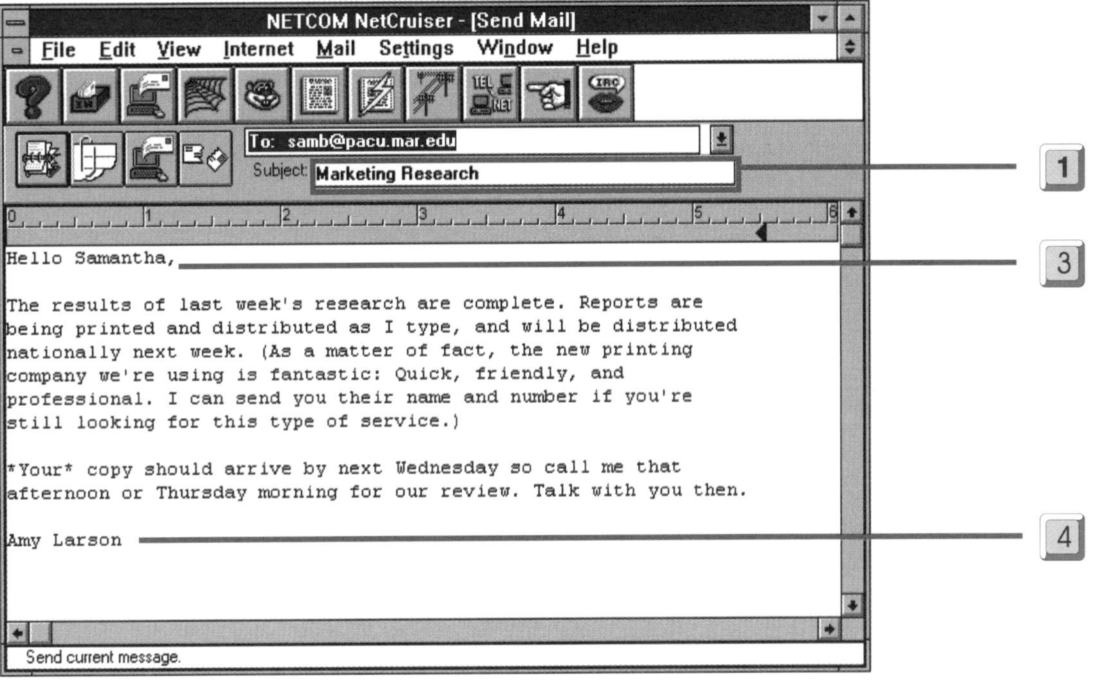

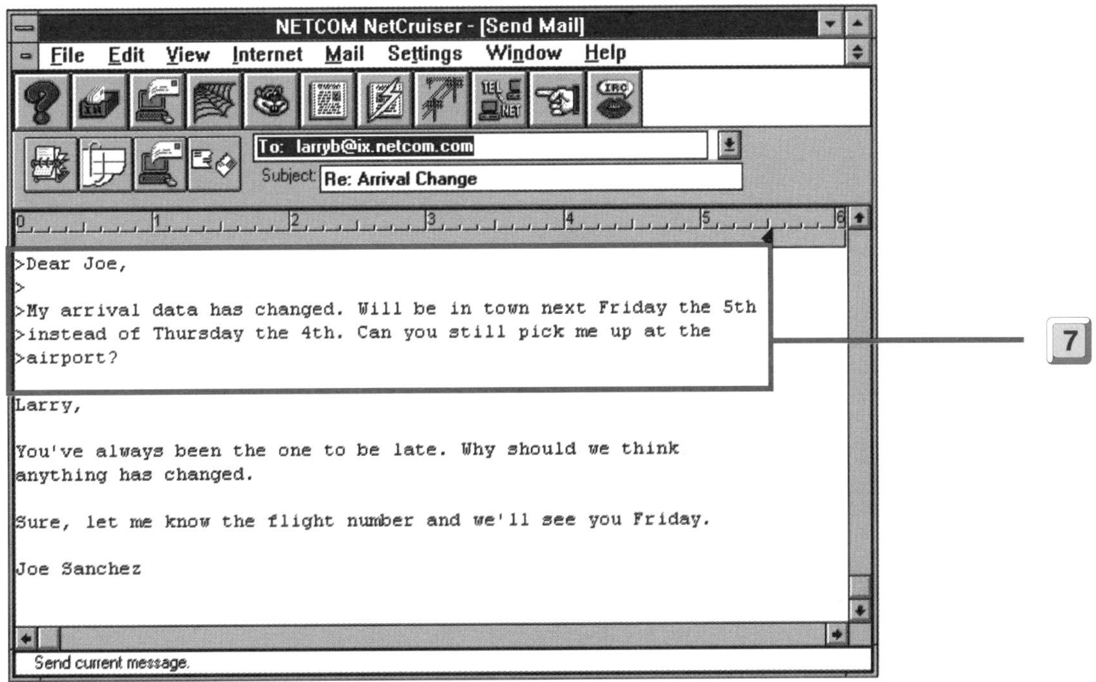

Getting Started

❖ Netiquette

In this lesson you will learn some unwritten etiquette guidelines to follow when using the Internet. The Internet's version of etiquette (Netiquette), refers to the unwritten rules of behavior on the Internet.

Guidelines

Here are some Netiquette guidelines to follow when using Email and other services:

1. **Insulting, degrading, or racist comments are not tolerated.** Messages ignoring this rule are said to be a "flame" and should be avoided at all costs. Delete messages containing this type of content and do not reply to them. Replying only makes matters worse and entices the sender.

2. **Email is not for advertising and get-rich-quick schemes.** Despite what some folks may say, the Internet was not formed for monetary gains. Unwanted and blatant advertising has been tried numerous times and condemned universally. You will, however, find specific areas on the Internet for this purpose, which is fine. The difference with these areas is that the user seeks them out on their own.

3. **It is acceptable to mention a company or product if you think it may help someone when it relates to the content of the message.** An example would be a company that has given you outstanding service, etc.

4. **Be subtle when using emphasis.** Many Email messages contain an *emphasis* on certain _points_. Emphasis is often enclosed in *asterisks* or _underlines_. Use your best judgment when adding emphasis. Also, major points may be given in upper case letters. Use these only when needed. A message or statement in all UPPER CASE IS CONSIDERED SHOUTING AND IN POOR TASTE.

Getting Started

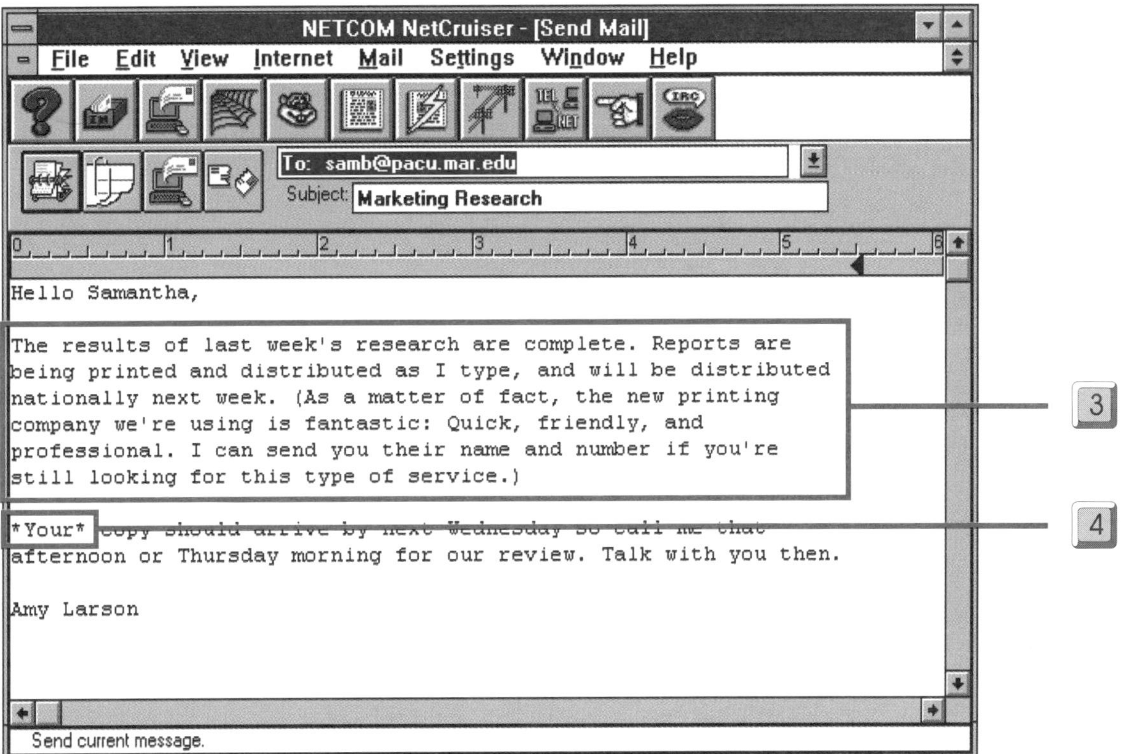

Insulting comments are not tolerated

Email is not for advertising

Be subtle when using emphasis

Getting Started

❖ Abbreviations and Emoticons

In this lesson you will learn how to save time by using Abbreviations and Emoticons.

Abbreviations

To save typing time and shorten postings, some users include abbreviations in their messages. Abbreviations represent common phrases and are delivered in upper case. Some examples include:

BTW	(By The Way)
OTOH	(On The Other Hand)
IMHO	(In My Humble Opinion)
IMO	(In My Opinion)
LOL	(Laughing Out Loud)
ROTFL	(Rolling On The Floor Laughing)
PMJI	(Pardon Me for Jumping In)
TIA	(Thanks In Advance)
FWIW	(For What It's Worth)
IYO	(In Your Opinion)

Emoticons

Others are not really abbreviations but are meant as a method for setting the tone of a sentence or an entire message. <G> for instance represents a "grin," and indicates sarcasm or states the message should be taken light-heartedly.

Emoticons are similar to abbreviations. They set the tone of a message or indicate the sender's "emotions."

The most common emoticon is the smiley, **:-)**. (Tilt your head to the left and view the symbol sideways, it resembles a smiley face.)

In contrast, **:-(** means sad. Others include: **;-)** a wink, and **:-o** a wow! or surprise.

Getting Started

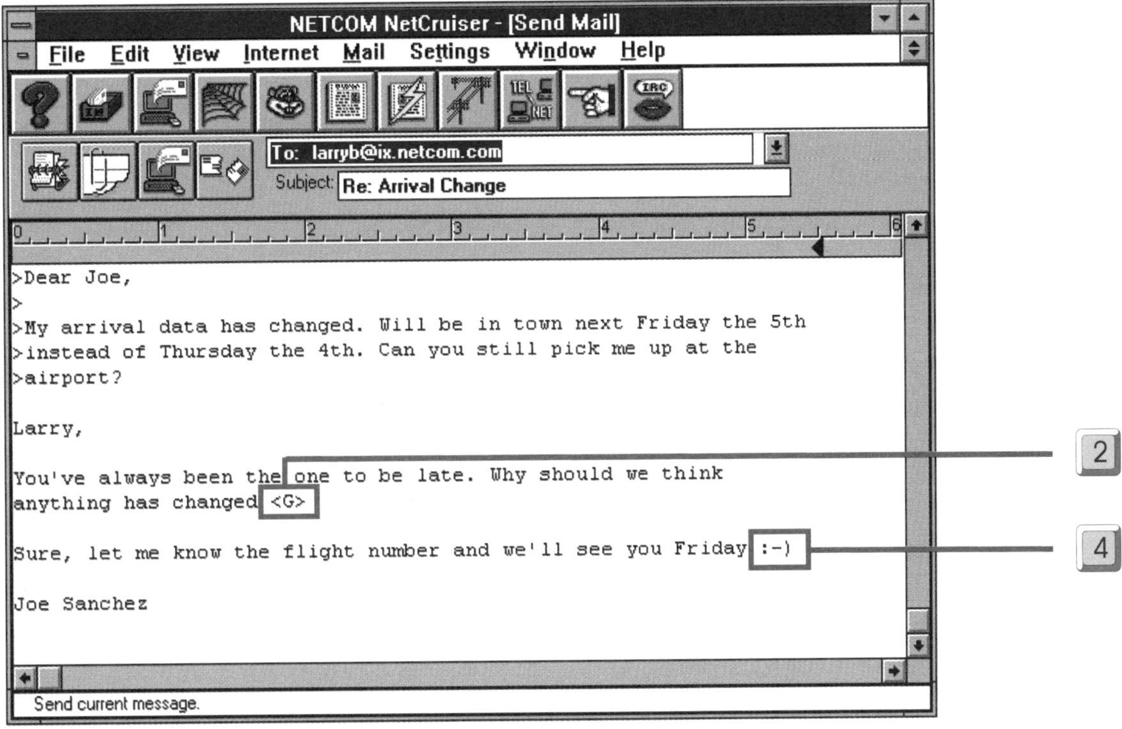

Use abbreviations and emoticons sparingly as they can make messages difficult to read. Also, excessive use of them is a sure sign of an Internet amateur.

Note: These Email Guidelines, Netiquette, Abbreviations, and Emoticons are not the "end all" for Internet behavior. Additional information is readily available on the Internet and in other publications.

Quick Reference Bar

<G> =
A grin

:-) =
A smiley face

:-(=
A sad face

;-) =
A wink

:-o =
A wow

INST

4

Addresses

❖ Understanding Internet Addresses

Addresses are the key to the Internet. Each connected computer has an address to note its location and allow connections to and from other computers. Addresses are used to send messages across the "net" to a specific user, as well as connect to Host computers for file retrieval and other services. This lesson provides further details of Internet addresses and assists in understanding their meaning.

Account Addresses

1 An address for an Internet account has two parts, separated by an @ sign. To the left of the @ is the User or Login name. To the right of the @ is the name of the Host computer for that account.

2 For example, take a look at the NETCOM address: johnd@.ix.netcom.com. "Johnd" could represent the user's name for registering the account, John Doe. While the remaining part represents the Host computer, "ix.netcom.com."

Host Computers

3 A large network consisting of multiple computers may be connected to the Internet, with one or all of those computers acting as a Host. For instance, one of the computers may have the address of: bigcomputer.bignetwork.com.us. To decipher the address, view it from right to left.

Domains and Zones

4 US is a geographic zone meaning the computer is in the United States. COM is a non-geographic zone meaning the computer is for commercial use. BIGNETWORK is the network Domain, and BIGCOMPUTER is a computer within the Domain. This naming system is referred to as the Domain Naming System (DNS). You may have noticed that ix.netcom.com does not have a geographic zone, and you'd be right. US is implied on many hosts within the states, but this may change soon, with more US zones being used.

Geographic Zones

Examples of other geographic zones: AU (Australia), CA (Canada), JP (Japan), SE (Sweden), ES (Spain), UK (United Kingdom [official code is GB]), NO (Norway), and FR (France).

Non-Geographic Zones

Examples of other non-geographic zones: EDU (Educational Institutions), GOV (Government bodies and departments), INT (International organizations), MIL (Military sites), NET (Network organizations), and ORG (Anything else not fitting one of the other zones).

IP Addresses

5 With this in mind, here is something you should be aware of: Host names are really a convenient way of referring to the Host computer's Internet Protocol Address, or IP Address. An IP Address is a unique number assigned to each Host computer on the Internet. The address is usually comprised of four numbers between one and 254, separated by periods. For example: 182.85.105.320. Luckily, most software automatically translates the Host name into it's corresponding IP Address, to keep you from having to also remember the numeric address. Note that having the IP Address may be useful in some situations so make note of it when it's available.

Addresses

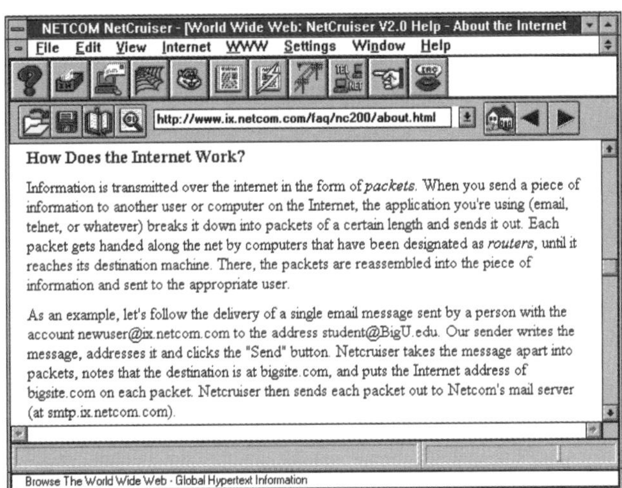

How Does the Internet Work?

Information is transmitted over the internet in the form of *packets*. When you send a piece of information to another user or computer on the Internet, the application you're using (email, telnet, or whatever) breaks it down into packets of a certain length and sends it out. Each packet gets handed along the net by computers that have been designated as *routers*, until it reaches its destination machine. There, the packets are reassembled into the piece of information and sent to the appropriate user.

As an example, let's follow the delivery of a single email message sent by a person with the account newuser@ix.netcom.com to the address student@BigU.edu. Our sender writes the message, addresses it and clicks the "Send" button. Netcruiser takes the message apart into packets, notes that the destination is at bigsite.com, and puts the Internet address of bigsite.com on each packet. Netcruiser then sends each packet out to Netcom's mail server (at smtp.ix.netcom.com).

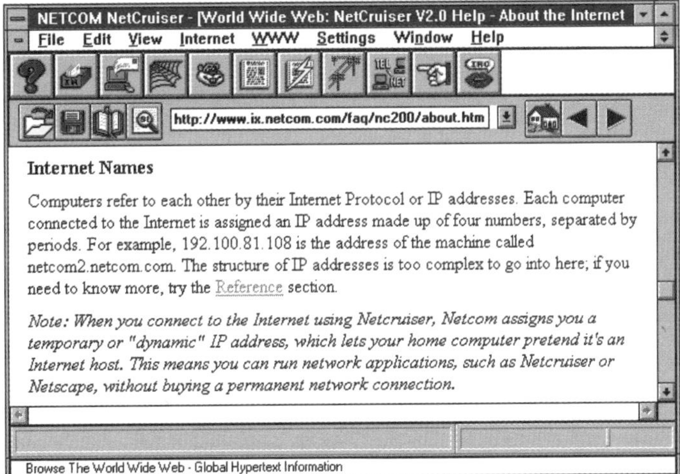

Internet Names

Computers refer to each other by their Internet Protocol or IP addresses. Each computer connected to the Internet is assigned an IP address made up of four numbers, separated by periods. For example, 192.100.81.108 is the address of the machine called netcom2.netcom.com. The structure of IP addresses is too complex to go into here; if you need to know more, try the Reference section.

Note: When you connect to the Internet using Netcruiser, Netcom assigns you a temporary or "dynamic" IP address, which lets your home computer pretend it's an Internet host. This means you can run network applications, such as Netcruiser or Netscape, without buying a permanent network connection.

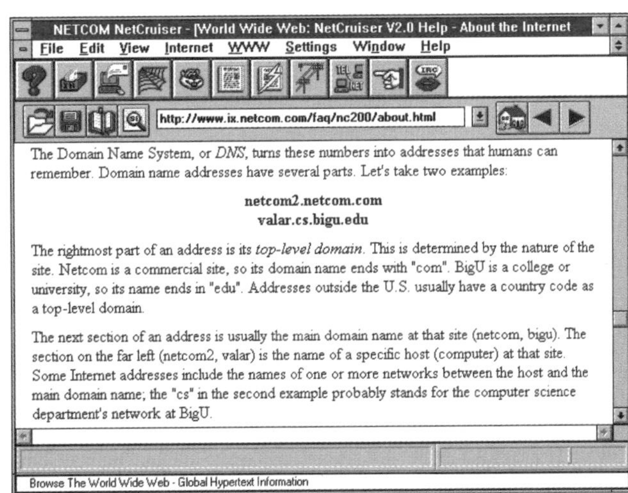

The Domain Name System, or *DNS*, turns these numbers into addresses that humans can remember. Domain name addresses have several parts. Let's take two examples:

netcom2.netcom.com
valar.cs.bigu.edu

The rightmost part of an address is its *top-level domain*. This is determined by the nature of the site. Netcom is a commercial site, so its domain name ends with "com". BigU is a college or university, so its name ends in "edu". Addresses outside the U.S. usually have a country code as a top-level domain.

The next section of an address is usually the main domain name at that site (netcom, bigu). The section on the far left (netcom2, valar) is the name of a specific host (computer) at that site. Some Internet addresses include the names of one or more networks between the host and the main domain name; the "cs" in the second example probably stands for the computer science department's network at BigU.

INST

4

Quick Reference Bar

An Internet account address consists of a User name and Host computer, separated by an "@"

Host computer names are deciphered from right to left

Computer names consist of geographic zones, non-geographic zones and domains

An IP Address consists of four sets of numbers separated by periods

Software translates the Host name to its IP Address

Electronic Mail

❖ Working with an Address Book

The NetCruiser Address Book stores the addresses of people and organizations you correspond with through Email. Entries store the recipients name and Email address that are inserted automatically when sending mail. Entries are managed easily. This lesson will show you how to add, edit or delete entries.

Starting NetCruiser

1. With Windows running, start NetCruiser. Open the NetCruiser group in Windows then double-click the **NetCruiser** icon. (To open the NetCruiser group, click **Window** then **NetCruiser**.)
2. Type your password in the Password: box; then click **Start Login**. An Internet connection is made.

A "Message From NETCOM" box may appear when first connecting. Read the message to be notified of important information from NETCOM. Click ***OK*** *afterward.*

Adding an Entry

3. Click **Internet**, then **Address Book**.
4. Click **New Entry**.
5. Type the recipient's name in the Name box. Now press **TAB** or click the **Email Address** box.
6. Type the Email address. Press **TAB** or click the **Comments** box.
7. Type in any comments for the recipient (optional). Click **OK**. The entry appears in the Address Book List. (When the list contains more entries than can be displayed, click the **vertical** scroll bar to see the additional entries.)
8. Repeat steps 4-7 for each entry.

Add entries for anyone you will correspond with via Email, if known at this time. Add them later if they are not. Include at least one entry of your own name and Email address. A message will be sent to yourself in lesson 7.

9. Click **Done**. Move on to the next lesson.

Electronic Mail

Quick Reference Bar

Click Internet, Address Book *to add entries*

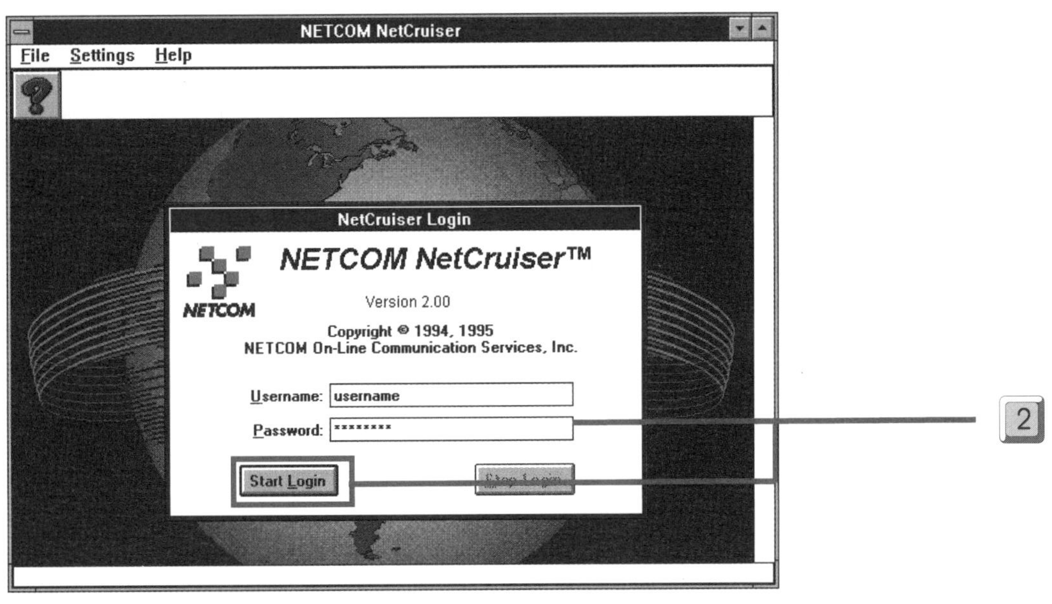

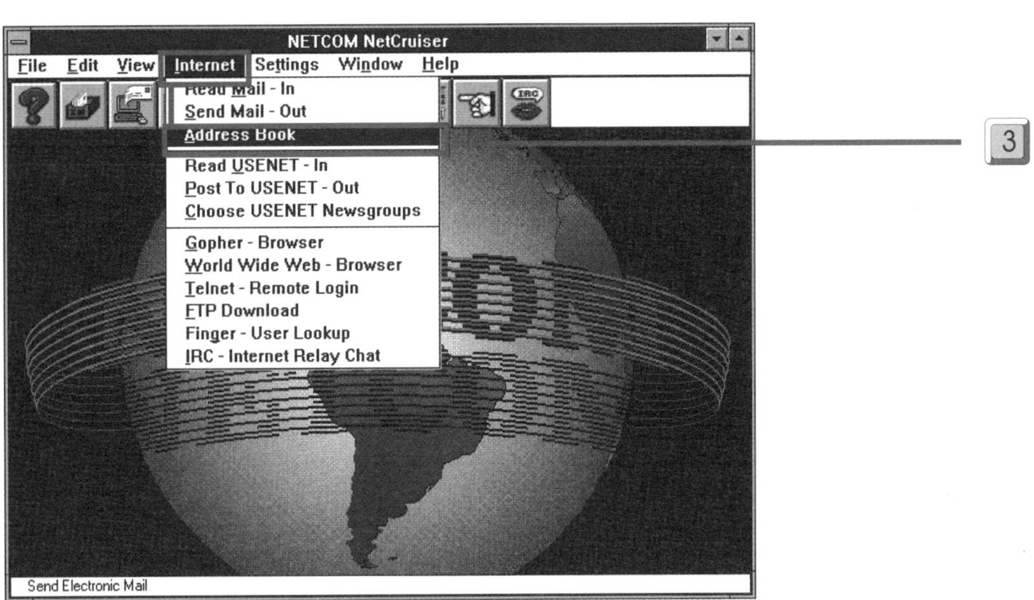

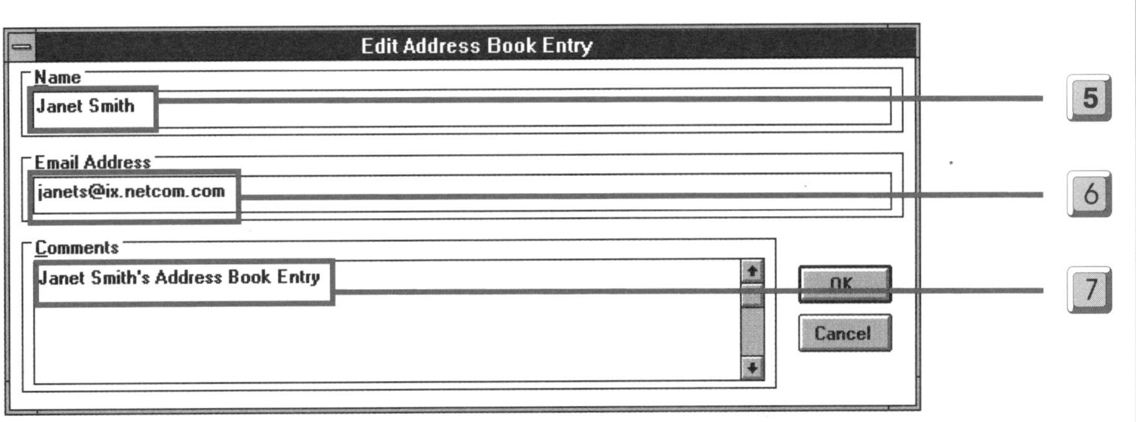

Electronic Mail

❖ Working with an Address Book

In this lesson you will learn how to edit and delete entries within an Address Book.

Editing an Entry

1. Click **Internet**, then **Address Book**. Now click the entry to edit.

2. Click **Edit**.

3. Make any desired changes. (The recipients Name or Email Address may change, or you may want to change the Comments field.)

4. Click **OK**.

> *Changes to the Name field are not instantly seen after clicking OK. To see the changes, click* ***Done****, then view the Address Book again (lesson 5, step 3).*

5. Click **Done**.

Deleting an Entry

6. Click **Internet**, then **Address Book**.

7. Click the entry to delete.

8. Click **Delete**, then **Done**.

> *To save usage time, feel free to disconnect from NETCOM at any time during the remaining lessons (preferably after the lesson has been completed). Click* ***File****,* ***Exit****, then* ***Yes****. Most lessons do, however, require a NETCOM connection, so reconnect before proceeding.*

Electronic Mail

Quick Reference Bar

Click Edit *to make changes to an entry*

Click Delete *to remove an entry*

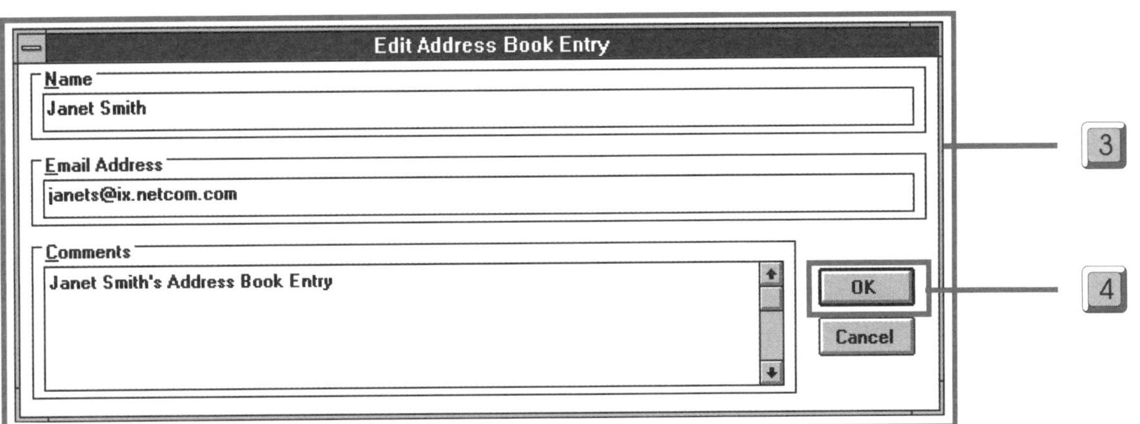

Electronic Mail

❖ Sending Email Messages

With the Address Book set, you're ready to send a message. In this lesson you will send a message to a single recipient or to multiple recipients, including yourself.

Selecting a Recipient

1. Click the **"Send Electronic Mail"** icon on the Toolbar. Or click **Internet**, then **Send Mail - Out**.

2. Click the recipient for the message in the **...Or Choose Address From Address Book** box. (Only if you are sending a real message to a real recipient. Otherwise choose your own name.)

3. Click **Use**.

   Address Book entries can also be added from this area. Fill in the "Enter Email Address Here" box; then click **Save**.

Including Others

4. To include others, click **Cc** in the **...Or Choose Address From Address Book** box, then click the recipient. Click **Use**. (Cc yourself if your name was not selected in step 2. You will receive a copy of the message and read it in the next lesson.)Click **OK**.

Entering a Subject

5. Type a descriptive entry in the Subject: box. Press **ENTER** to move to the message area.

6. Type in the message. For a larger view of the message area, click the **up arrow** at the top right corner of the Send Mail window. The window is now in full-screen view mode.

*To change the font size, click **Mail**, then **Font Size**. Now click the new size. Regarding word wrap, this occurs at 72 characters as set by the indicator arrow below the ruler. To move the word wrap, click the **Indicator** and keep the mouse held down, then drag it to the desired location. Word wrap may need to be between 60-65 characters to assure readability on some systems. A font size of 10 with a word wrap of 5-5 1/2 inches should do for these instances.*

Sending a Message

7. Click the **"Send current message"** icon on the Mail window Toolbar. If the window is in full-screen view, a "Sending message..." box appears until the message is sent. If in windowed view, a "Sending message..." icon appears at the bottom of the screen until the message is sent.

   If you want to cancel a message before sending, click the **Control** button at the top left of the Mail window, then click **Close**. Click **Yes** to cancel. Sent messages are saved to your local hard disk in the \Netcom\Mail\Outbox subdirectory. Occasionally deleting these files will free up disk space. (Be sure the messages are not out of sequence afterward.)

Signature Files

8. You can automatically include a signature at the end of each message. Signatures usually contain a person's name, Email address and company information, but may also contain a simple quote or saying as a touch of style. Signature files need to be basic ASCII (text) files with the name of MAIL.SIG. Create with the Windows Notepad or another text editor, then store the file in the \Netcom directory. (See Appendix C for an example.)

Electronic Mail

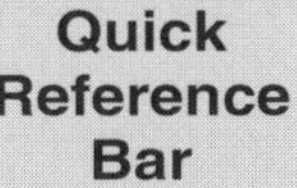

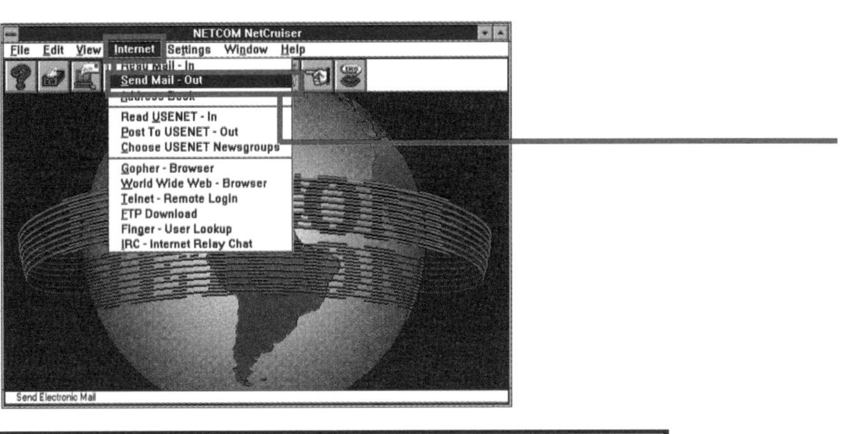

1

Click the "send..." icon to send mail

Click Mail, Font Size, Point Number *to change font size*

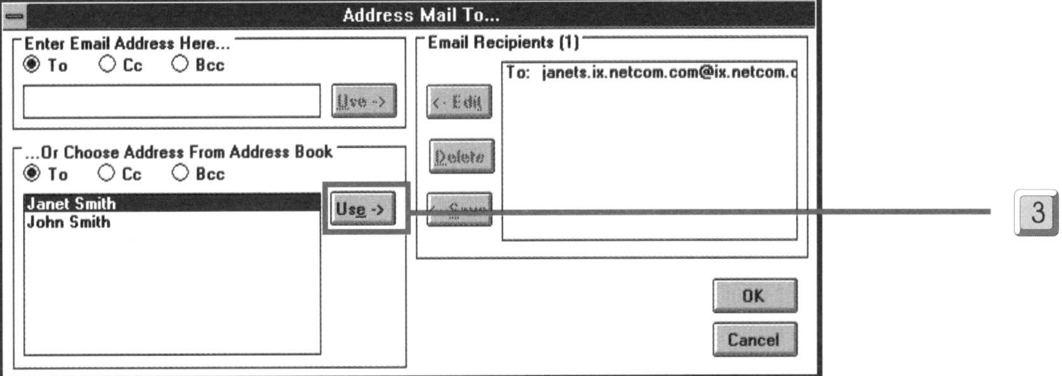

3

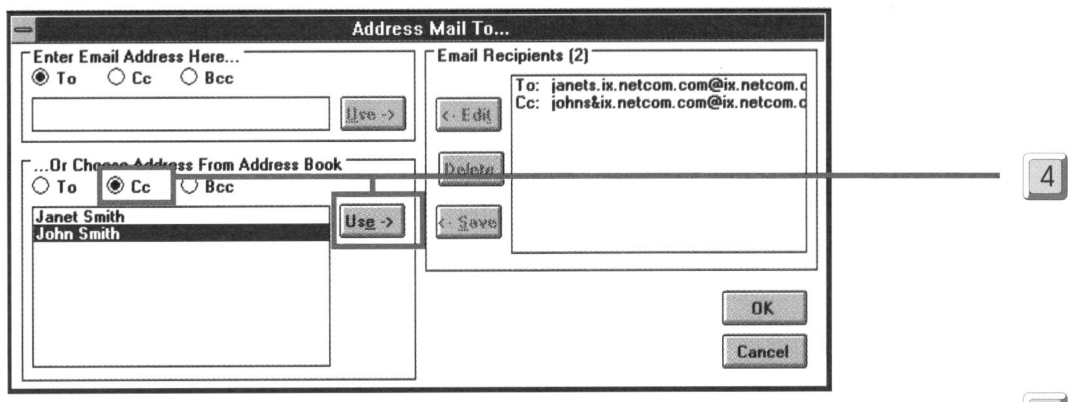

4

7

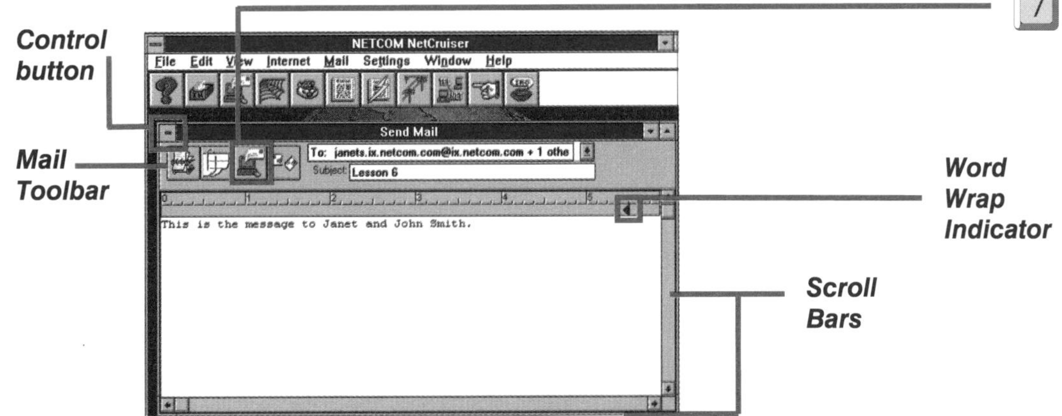

INST

8

Electronic Mail

❖ Receiving Email Messages

One of the most rewarding parts of Email is reading your messages. This lesson will show you how to read, reply, forward and save received messages.

Starting "Read

1. Click the **"In" box** icon on the Toolbar; or click **Internet**, then **Read Mail - In**.

2. The "Inbox" is selected. Click **OK**. (Click the **"Saved Mail"** selection when reading saved messages.)

3. Change to the full-screen view. Click the **up arrow** at the top right of the "Read Mail:New Mail" window.

Reading a Message

4. Double-click the message sent in lesson 7; or single-click the message, then click the **"Read next selected message"** icon. The message appears in the lower pane of the window. Click the **vertical** scroll bar of this pane when text exists but is not visible.

From here you can reply, forward and (or) save the message. To reply, click the **"Reply to current message"** icon. To forward, click the **"Forward current message"** icon. To save, click the **"Save current message"** icon. Saved messages are moved to the "Saved Mail" area. To see them, click the **Drop-down arrow** in the "Inbox" area then click **Saved Mail**. Saved mail is also stored as files on the local hard disk in the \Netcom\Mail subdirectory. Unlike sent messages, these files are removed from the disk when deleted in the "Saved Mail" list.

When multiple messages exist, click each message to read while holding down the CTRL key. Now click the ***"Read next selected message"*** *icon. (Or click the starting point of the messages to read and keep the mouse held down.) Now drag the mouse to select continuous messages. Now click the* ***"Read next selected message"*** *icon.*

Changing the Font Size

5. Change the font size of the text. Click **Mail**, **Fonts**, then **9 Point**. (Text of some messages extends to the right of the viewable area. Moving to a full-screen view and lowering the font size may help when this occurs.) Change back to 10 Point if you like.

When replying, click **Yes** to include the original message. Now edit the message to include only necessary references. References usually go at the beginning of the message with > (greater-than signs) preceding each line. The reply then follows the reference. To include another on the reply, click the **"Enter Mail To address"** icon. Cc is already selected. Click the **Name**, **Use**, then **OK**. Now click the **"Send current message"** icon.

Saving and Deleting Email

6. Save the message. Click the **"Save current message"** icon, then **OK**.

7. Delete the message. Click the **"Delete current message"** icon.

A message must be displayed in the lower pane to be saved or printed. However, it does not need to be displayed to be deleted. To delete a non-displayed message, click the message in the top pane, then click the **"Delete..."** icon. To delete multiple messages, click each message while holding down the CTRL key. Now delete as usual. Messages in the "Saved Mail" area are deleted through the same process.

Electronic Mail

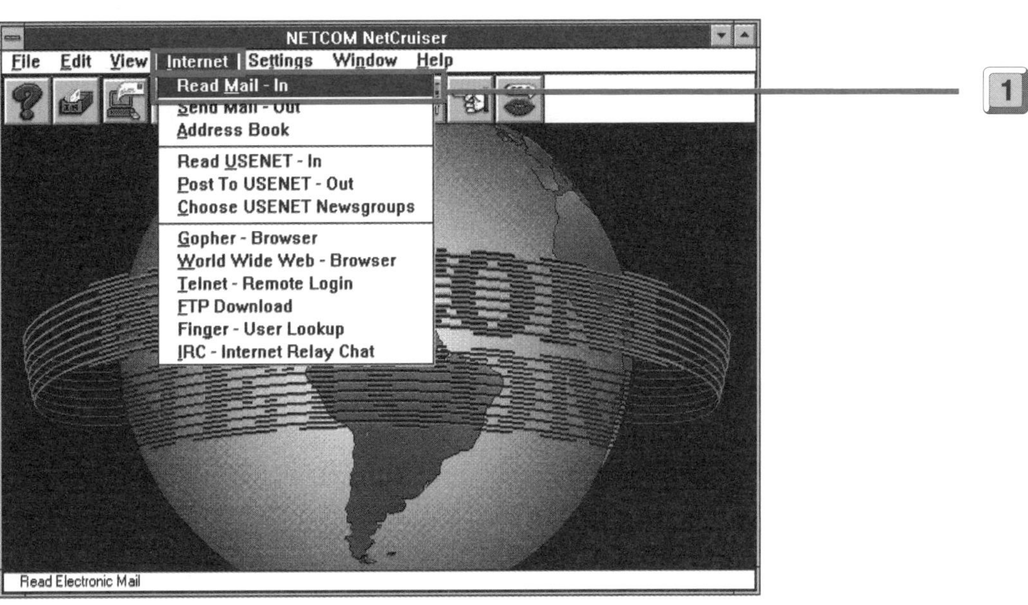

1

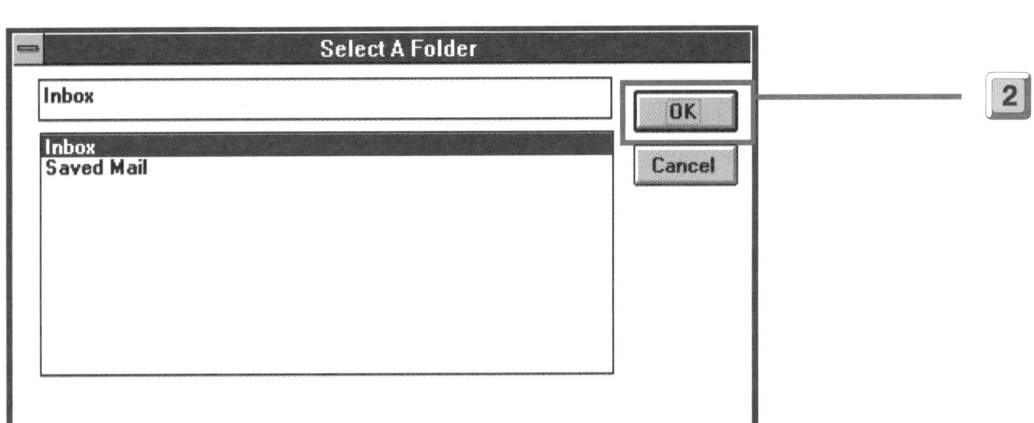

2

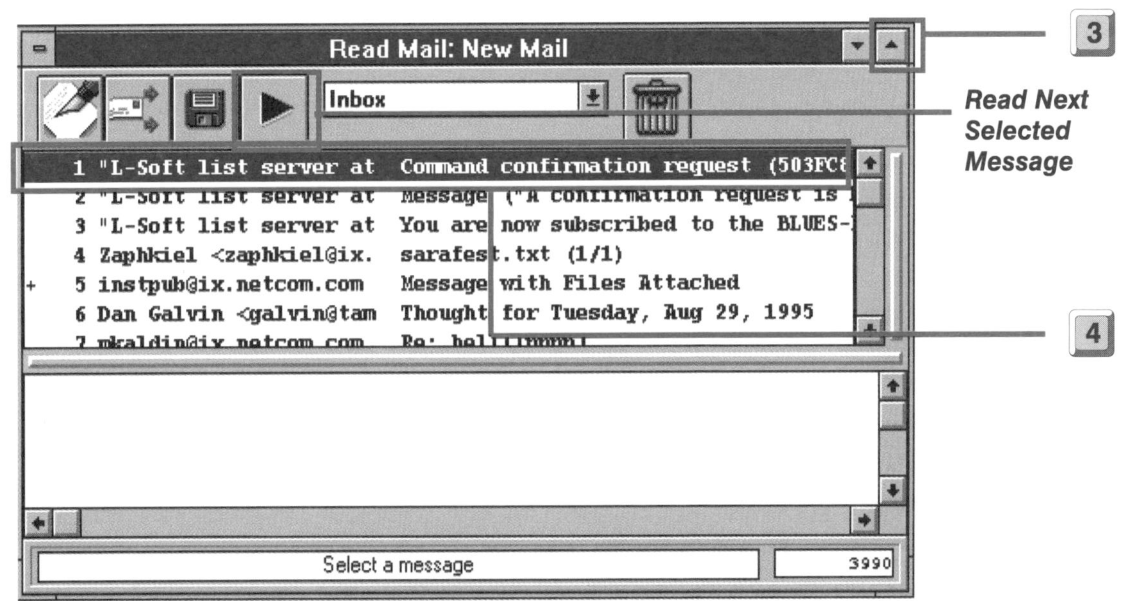

3

Read Next Selected Message

4

INST

8

Quick Reference Bar

Click the "Read..." Icon to read mail

Click Mail, Font Size, Point Number *to change font size*

Click File, Print Message *to send a message to the printer*

Press CTRL+F4 *to close "Read Mail"*

Electronic Mail

❖ File Attachments

In this lesson you will learn about sending a file or multiple files and attaching files to a text message.

Now that you know how to type a message from the keyboard and send it to someone on the Internet, what about sending a file? Well, the Internet and NetCruiser's mail program support file attachments. You can attach files to a text message or send a file or multiple files alone.

Limitations do exist when sending files. The following is a list of those limitations:

ASCII and Binary Files

1 The Internet only supports basic seven-bit ASCII text; text entered from the characters on a standard keyboard. Each ASCII character is represented by seven bits of digital information. Binary files on the other hand are made up of eight-bit characters. Examples of binary files are:

Executable files (.EXE and .COM)
Graphic files (.BMP and .GIF)
Sound files (.WAV and .AU)
Document files (.DOC and .WRI)

Converting Binary Files

2 To send binary files across the Internet they are first converted to ASCII seven-bit format. Two common methods are used to convert binary files, MIME (Multipurpose Internet Mail Exchange) and Uuencode. Once at the receiving end the files need to be converted back to their original eight-bit binary state. (Once converted to ASCII, the file is larger than its binary counterpart.)

MIME and Uuencode

3 NetCruiser's mail program fully supports MIME. Meaning: attached files are converted automatically behind the scenes and without interaction from the user. As long as the receiving end supports MIME, nothing more needs to be done in most cases. If the receiving mail program does not support MIME, the MIME Munpack program can be used on the attached file. Munpack converts the file back to binary format.

4 Attaching a file is not a problem on your end but what if you receive a file converted to ASCII with the Uuencode program? Use the Decode program to convert the file to binary. You can download (send to your local computer) the MIME and Uuencode utility programs from the Internet. A later lesson will take you through this process.

To send a file, click the **"Add Attachment "** *icon in the Send Mail window, then select the file.*

To see if a received file needs to be converted, save the file then try to use it. If the file is not usable, run the Munpack or Decode program to convert the file, depending on the file's type. (Try both programs if the type is unknown.)

Electronic Mail

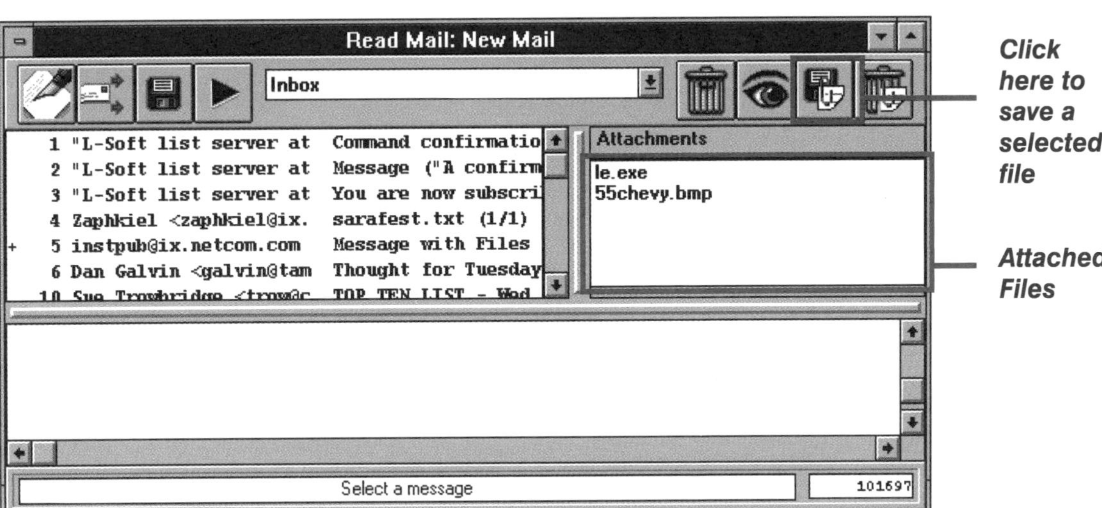

Click here to save a selected file

Attached Files

To save a binary file showing in the "Attachments" window (above), click the file to select it, then click the **"Save..."** icon.

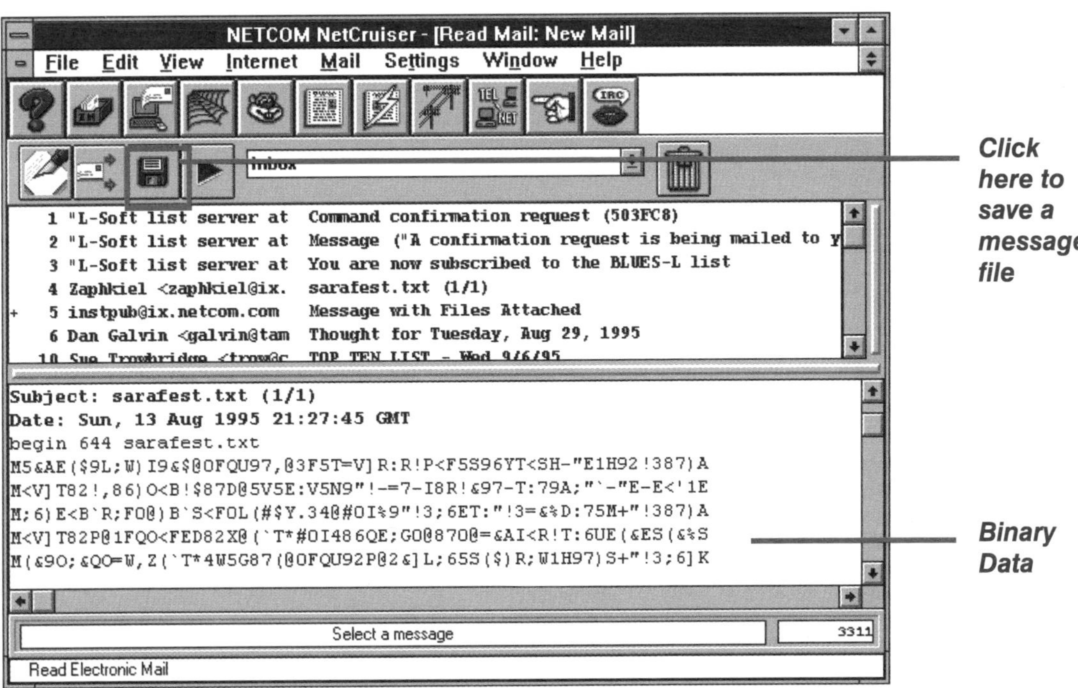

Click here to save a message file

Binary Data

To save a binary file showing in the message area (above), click the **"Save current..."** icon. The file is saved to the \netcom\mail subdirectory with a name consisting of numbers and a .MSG extension. By default, the decode program requires a .UUE extension. Rename accordingly.

INST

9

Quick Reference Bar

The Internet supports ASCII text in messages, not binary files

Binary files must be converted to ASCII

Use Munpack or Decode to convert an ASCII file to binary

INST

10

Usenet Newsgroups

Newsgroup Names and Guidelines

In this lesson you will learn about Usenet Newsgroups and the guidelines for using them.

Usenet refers to a medium supporting numerous discussion groups called Newsgroups. Newsgroups allow the exchange of information and ideas between users around the globe. First developed for the exchange of technical information, Newsgroups have grown to include non-technical subjects like news items, social interests and hobbies. No matter what the topic you can probably find an associated Newsgroup.

Think of Newsgroups as an organized form of Email, with messages being sent to multiple users instead of a single recipient and with a focused interest. Users can simply "browse" a Newsgroup for information or fully participate by sending their own articles and replying to others. (Messages are considered "articles" in the world of Newsgroups.) Most groups are open for any type of posting but some are moderated. Postings to a moderated Newsgroup will take longer to appear as they need to first go through the moderator.

Newsgroup Names

Newsgroup names allow for easy identification. Take the Newsgroup **alt.arts.movies** for example. You instantly get an idea of the group's topics. The first part of the group is its identifier, **alt**, meaning it's an alternative Newsgroup. Following are Newsgroup identifiers to be aware of: 1. biz (Business) 2. rec (Recreational) 3. news (General news) 4. soc (Social) 5. sci (Scientific) 6.talk (Debate oriented) 7.comp (Computers)
8. alt (Alternative tends to be less formal and has a smaller distribution)
9. misc (Doesn't fall into one of the other categories)

Newsgroup Guidelines

The issues relating to File Attachments, Guidelines and Netiquette for Email are also pertinent to Newsgroups (refer to the "Getting Started" section if you need a refresher). There are however some additions relating to Newsgroups.

1 **Browse a Newsgroup for some time before posting an article.** Get an idea of the tone and style of the group before sending or replying to an article.

2 **Check the FAQ file before posting questions.** FAQs, or Frequently Asked Questions, are usually available on each Newsgroup. Check these documents before posting your question. Your answer may be found there.

3 **Avoid cross posting.** Cross posting refers to sending an article to more than one group, sometimes called "spamming." This is considered poor manners by most users. If you do want to cross post, make sure the subject matter is relevant to each group.

4 **Be sure your message has something to say.** A few words in a reply simply stating that you agree or disagree with a point is not in everyone's best interest. Check that the message has something to add to the discussion before sending.

5 **Do not send "test" messages to a group.** Newsgroups have been around for a while and it's safe to assume the system works. Send any test messages only to a test group, like **alt.test**, **misc.test** etc.

6 Other information is available in the Newsgroup **news.announce.newusers**, which you will locate in lesson 11.

Usenet Newsgroups

INST

10

Quick Reference Bar

biz = *Business*

rec= *Recreational*

news= *General News*

soc= *Social*

sci= *Scientific*

talk= *Debate Oriented*

comp= *Computer*

alt= *Alternative*

misc= *Doesn't fit a category*

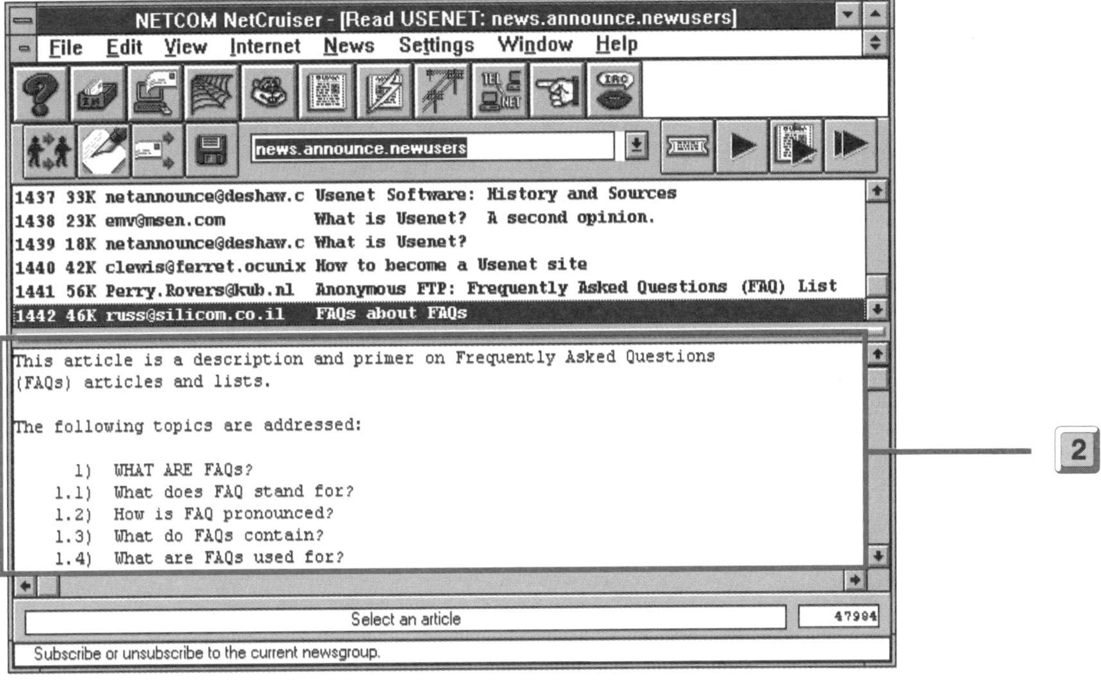

2

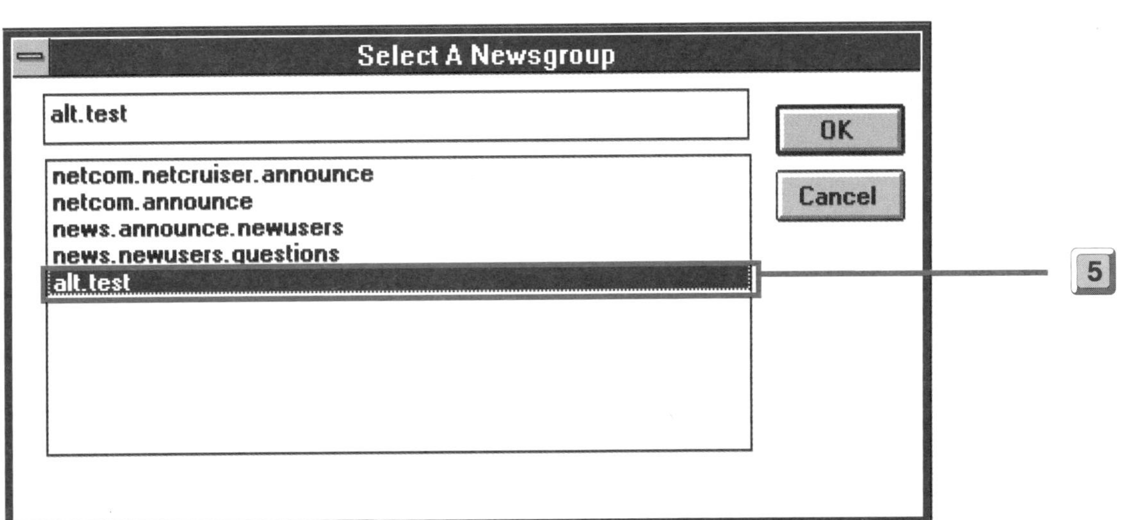

5

INST

11

Usenet Newsgroups

❖ Choosing Usenet Newsgroups

With a background of Usenet under your belt, it's time to subscribe to the Newsgroups that interest you. Subscribing to a group will add it to a list, and from that list allow easy access for reading its articles.

Choosing a Category

1. Click **Internet**, then **Choose USENET Newsgroups**.

2. Click the **Help/Reference** icon in the Categories area. (Click the **up** or **down arrow** on the vertical scroll bar to see different areas of the window.)

3. Click the **down arrow** on the vertical scroll bar to see the items in the selected category box.

Choosing a Group

4. Click a group you want to add, then click **Subscribe**. The group appears in the "My Reading List" box to the right.

5. Repeat steps 3& 4 for each desired group.

> *Here's a group that will answer many questions regarding Newsgroups: **news.answers**. Subscribing to this group is recommended. Then, check this group for FAQs (Frequently Asked Questions) relating to various groups (most of them post their FAQs to this group). Other groups providing answers: rec.answers, sci.answers, soc.answers, and talk.answers.*

6. Click the **up arrow** on the vertical scroll bar to view the Categories area. Click another category that interests you or click **All** to see everything.

7. Repeat steps 3 & 4 for each desired group.

8. Click **OK** when done.

> *This is not the complete list of Newsgroups, new ones are created frequently nor is this the only way to subscribe. If you come across the address of another group that you want to subscribe to, use the address in the "Read USENET - In" command, move to the group, then use the Subscribe command. More about this in the next lesson.*

Usenet Newsgroups

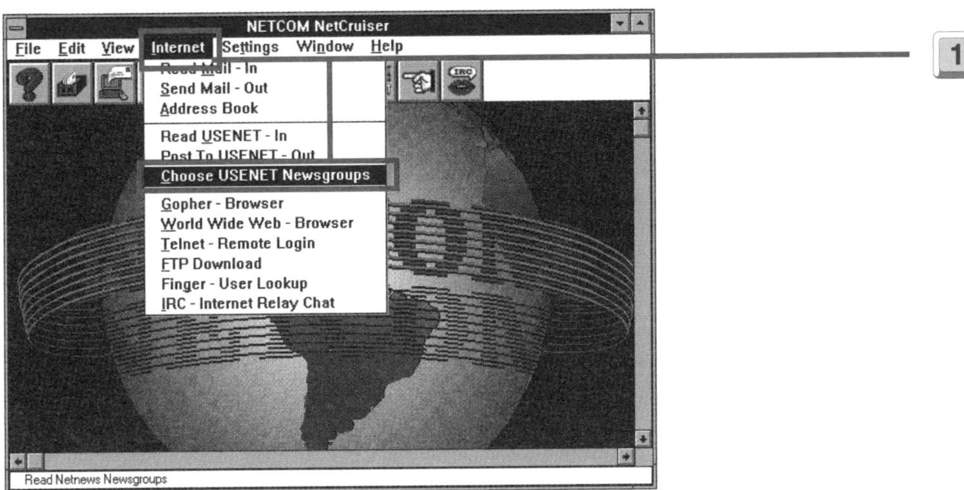

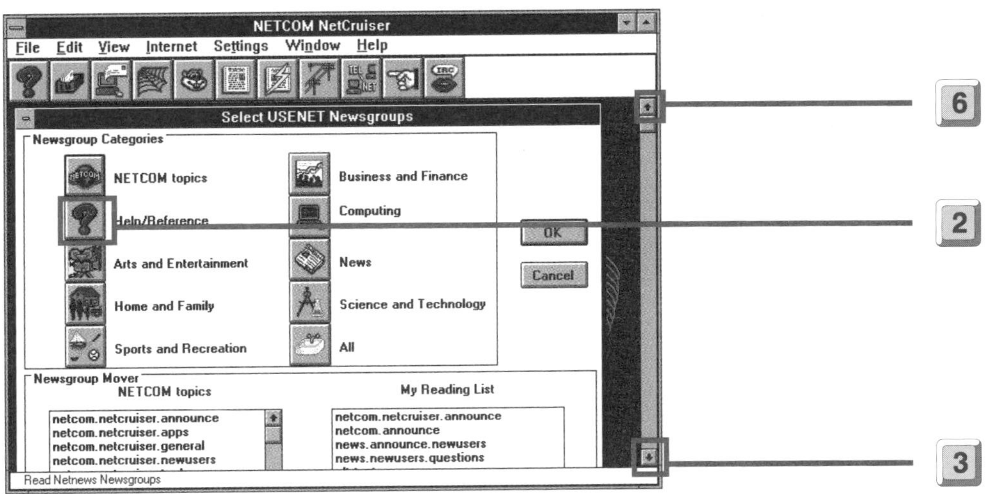

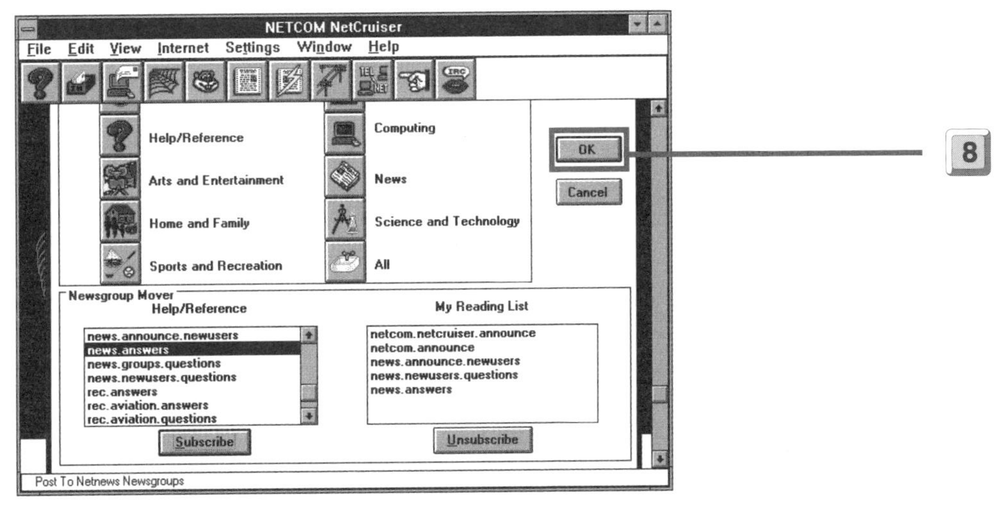

Click Internet, then Choose USENET Newsgroups to subscribe to listed groups

Click Subscribe to add a selected group

Click Unsubscribe to remove a selected group

INST

12

Usenet Newsgroups

❖ Browsing Newsgroup Articles

Okay, let's move to one of the subscribed groups and browse some of its articles. This lesson will show how to connect to the "news.newusers.questions" group and find additional information about Usenet. Connect to the other groups through the same process with the appropriate group selected.

Selecting a Group to Browse

1. Click the **"Read Netnews Newsgroups"** icon on the Toolbar; or click **Internet**, then **Read USENET - In**.

2. Click the **"news.newusers.questions"** group, then click **OK**. (Click the **down arrow** on the vertical scroll bar if this group is not visible.)

3. Select the **"First Article To Read."** Click the **left arrow** in this box to move to the lowest number available; or click the box to the right of the "(minimum)" box then type the minimum number.

Entering a Range of Articles

4. Select the **"Last Article To Read."** Click the **right arrow** in this box to move to the highest number available; or click the box to the right of the "(maximum)" box then type the maximum number. (400 is the most available at one time.)

5. Click **OK**. The articles within the set range appear and are selected for browsing.

> ℹ *Look for the following articles in this Newsgroup: "Rules for Posting to Usenet," "A Primer on How to Work with the Usenet Community," "Answers to Frequently Asked Questions about Usenet," Emily Postnews Answers Your Questions on Netiquette," and "Hints for Writing Style for the Usenet." If not available check for them frequently.*

Moving to the Next Article

6. Click the **"Read next selected article"** icon on the "Read USENET" window. (Change to full-screen view if you like. Click the **up arrow** at the top right of the window.)

7. Save the article. Click the **"Save current article"** icon, then click **OK**. Saved articles are stored as files on the local hard disk, in the \Netcom\News subdirectory. Naming pattern is 00000001.msg, 00000002.msg etc. Rename the files for clarity if desired.

8. Read the next article (assuming another one is available). Click the **"Read next selected article"** icon. You can continue to read all selected articles or manually select which articles to read, as explained for Email in a previous lesson.

9. Close the Newsgroup when done. Click the **Control** button, then **Close**.

Closing a Newsgroup

> ℹ *To move to an unlisted group that you haven't subscribed to, click the* **"Read Newnews Newsgroups"** *icon on the Toolbar; or click* **Internet**, *then* **Read USENET - In**. *Now click* **Cancel**. *Next, click the empty Newsgroup box, then type the name of the group. Now click the* **"Subscribe to Newsgroup"** *icon.*

Usenet Newsgroups

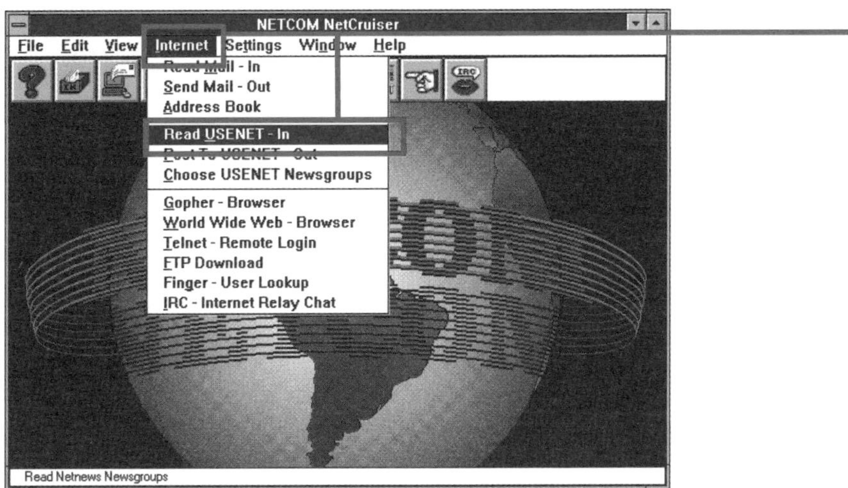

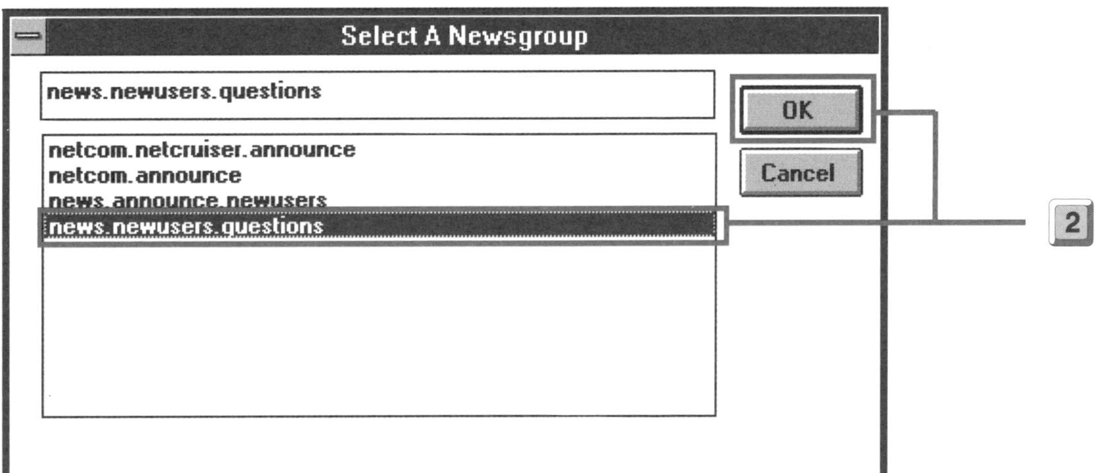

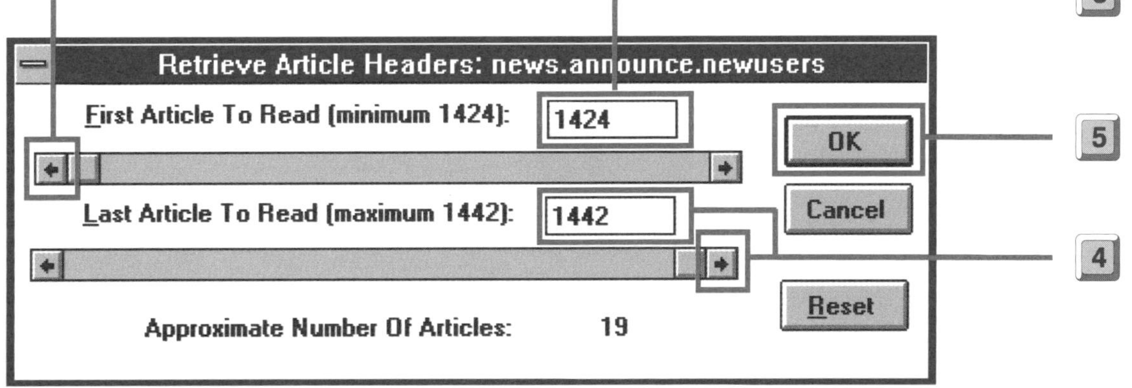

Quick Reference Bar

Click Internet, Read Usenet - In *to browse a group*

Click the "Read Next..." *Icon to read selected articles*

Click File, Print Article *to send an article to the printer*

Press CTRL+F4 *to close "Read USENET"*

13 Usenet Newsgroups

❖ Posting a Newsgroup Article

In this lesson you will learn how to send an article to a "test" group. Later, use the same process to send to a real group with the appropriate group selected.

Entering a Group for Posting

1. Click the **"Post To Netnews Newsgroups"** icon on the Toolbar.
2. Click the **Newsgroups:** area. Type **alt.test** (lower case).
3. Press **ENTER** or click the **Subject:** line.
4. Type **Test Only; Ignore**.

   For most test Newsgroups, including "Ignore" in the Subject line will avoid receiving a reply message automatically. If you do want to receive a reply leave "Ignore" out.

Entering Text for an Article

5. Press **ENTER**. Type: **This is a test article to the alt.test group**.

   When sending an article it is not necessary to type the entire text while on-line with an Internet connection. You can write the text in another Windows' program, then copy and paste the text to the message area. After copying the text in the other program, click **Edit** then **Paste**. Additionally, signature files can be used with Newsgroup articles, just as with Email. Create the same type of file but with the name: NEWS.SIG, stored in the \Netcom directory. (See Appendix C for an example.)

Sending an Article

6. Click **Send**. A "Usenet Posting Tips" window appears. Read the message, then click **Yes**.

   After becoming a true Usenet "wiz" you can bypass this message. Edit the NETCOM.INI file in the \Windows directory with your favorite text editor, Notepad for instance. Move to the [User] section and add the line: ShowUsenetTips=False. (Minus the period.) Save the file. Restart NetCruiser to make effective.

Reading an Article

7. View the test article. Click the **"Read Netnews Newsgroups"** icon on the Toolbar.
8. Click **Cancel**, then click the empty box. Type **alt.test**, then press **ENTER.**
9. Select the **"First Article To Read."** Click the **left arrow** in this box to move to the lowest number available; or click the box to the right of the "(minimum)" box, then type the minimum number. (The message should be near the maximum below). Set accordingly.
10. Select the **"Last Article To Read."** Click the **right arrow** in this box to move to the highest number available; or click the box to the right of the "(maximum)" box, then type the maximum number. (Set to the highest number possible.)
11. Click **OK**. The articles within the set range appear and are selected for viewing.
12. Locate then double-click the message. Click the **up** or **down** arrow on the vertical scroll bar if necessary.
13. Close the Newsgroup when done. Click the **Control** button, then **Close**.

Usenet Newsgroups

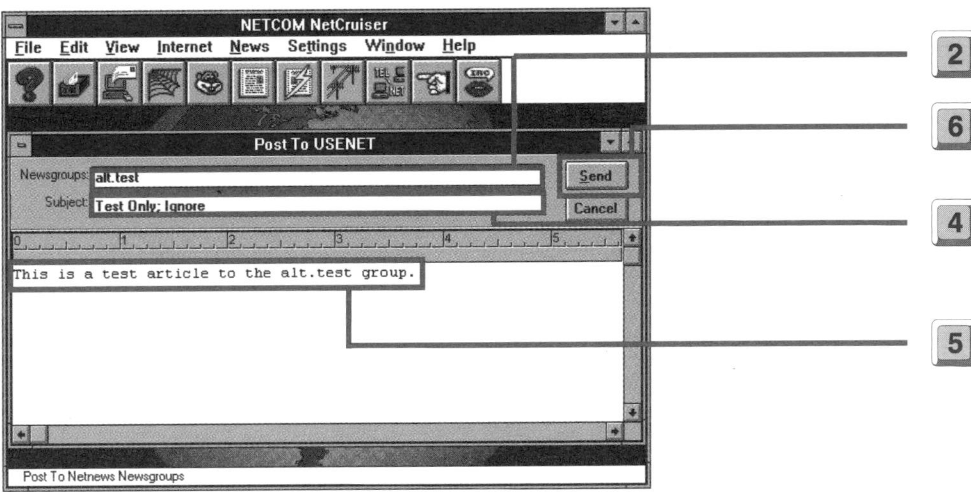

USENET Posting Tips

STOP

Before you post to Usenet, read the followings :

1. Don't post advertisements to any group which doesn't specifically allow them in the FAQ or charter. Almost all of the groups which allow ads are in the biz.*hierarchy. Most of the *.forsale groups don't allow ads - they are for single "garage-sale" transactions between private individuals only!

An advertisement is any post which makes money for the sender, directly or indirectly.

2. Regional groups, such as ba.general or austin.jobs, are for posts that relate to that local area only! If you want to say something to the whole country/world, post to a nonregional group.

3. Only post to the groups which best suit your article. Usenet is organized by subject, and no message is related to more than a few groups.

4. "Make-Money-Fast" chain letters are not appropriate for any group, and may be illegal. Do not post them or respond to them.

Are you sure you want to post your message to thousands of computer systems around the world?

Yes No

6

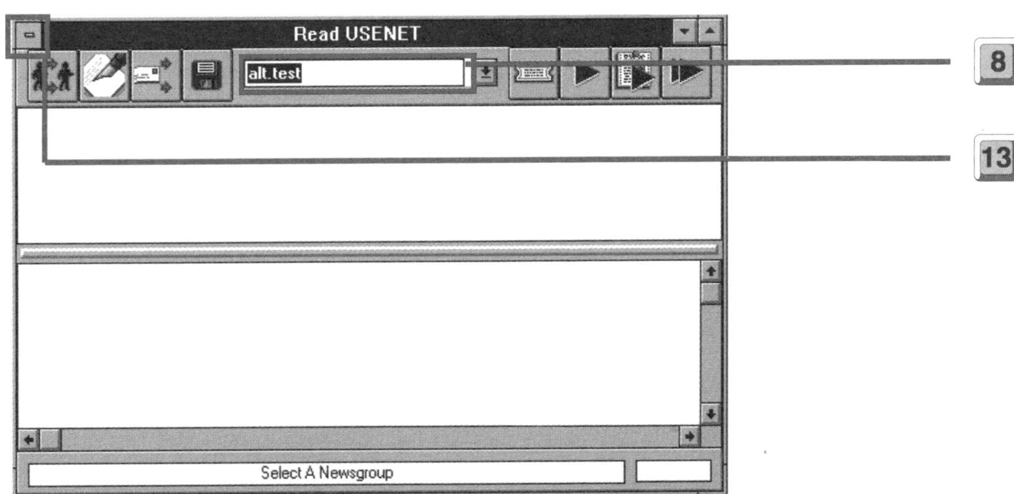

Quick Reference Bar

Click the "Post To..." icon to send an article

Press CTRL+F4 *to close "Read USENET"*

Mailing Lists

❖ Types of Mailing Lists

In this lesson you will learn about the different types of mailing lists and what they have to offer. You will also learn how to send commands to LISTSERV and to send messages to a mailing list.

An Email account truly opens up your options for the Internet, one of which are mailing lists. These lists deal with a specific subject or topic. Messages relating to the topic are sent to everyone subscribed to the list. Think of mailing lists as a function similar to both Email and Newsgroups. Similar to Email in that the information is retrieved from NetCruiser's Mail program, and comparable to UseNet groups in that the information shared is focused.

Types of Mailing Lists

Different types of mailing lists exist. Examples include the TFTD-L (Thought For The Day) list which is a one-way interaction. A "thought for the day" is sent to each subscriber with no information being sent from the subscribers to the list. (There may be times when sending a message to the administrator of this type of list is necessary.)

Another type of list is one that functions like a newspaper or a magazine subscription. Articles are published through the list in certain intervals, weekly, bi-weekly, monthly, etc. These types of lists may or may not encourage submissions from its subscribers.

A third and most common type of mailing list is one that acts as a mail "exploder." Mail sent to the list's address is forwarded (or exploded) to each subscriber of the list. Messages can range from the most basic in content to a highly debated discussion with many subscribers contributing. Sending messages is encouraged with this type of list. In fact, this is their main purpose; exchanging information, thoughts, ideas and questions freely.

List Managers

List managers are used to subscribe and signoff of a mailing list and to attain other pertinent data, such as a "list" of mailing lists to choose from. These managers are actually software run on a Host computer that monitor and send mailing list information. You can access these managers by sending Email to their appropriate Host address. Two of the most popular list managers are LISTSERV and Majordoma. The following three lessons deal with the LISTSERV manager, and show you how to Subscribe to and Signoff of a mailing list, and how to attain other mailing list information.

List Manager Commands

Sending Mail to LISTSERV
Commands are sent to the LISTSERV Host through its address, LISTSERV@TAMVM1.TAMU.EDU. Use this address when sending commands to subscribe, signoff, etc. to different mailing lists. This address should not be used when sending messages to mailing list subscribers.

Messages to Mailing Lists

Sending Messages to a Mailing List
Mailing lists have a separate address. For example, the address for the TFTD-L list is TFTD-L@TAMVM1.TAMU.EDU. Use this type of address when sending messages to the mailing list. (This is an example. Remember that the TFTD-L list is not an "exploding" type list.) Any list you subscribe to will have a similar type of address.

Mailing Lists

Quick Reference Bar

Mail is sent to each subscriber of a mailing list

List managers are used to "Subscribe" and "Signoff" a mailing list

Mail is sent to the mailing list's address

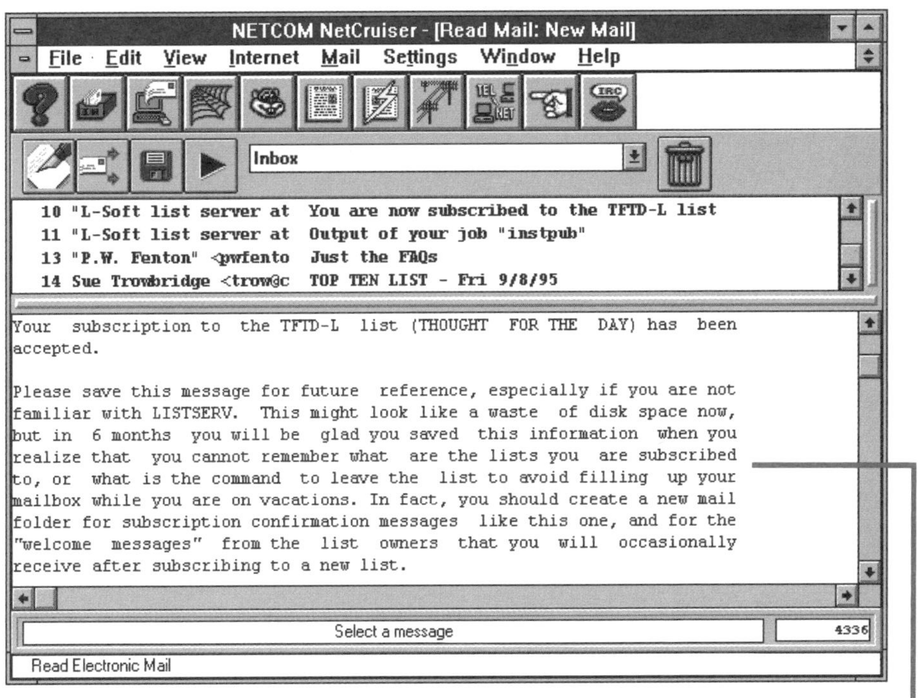

Responses to a "Subscribe" command

NETCOM NetCruiser - [Read Mail: New Mail]
File Edit View Internet Mail Settings Window Help
Inbox

```
10 "L-Soft list server at You are now subscribed to the TFTD-L list
11 "L-Soft list server at Output of your job "instpub"
13 "P.W. Fenton" <pwfento Just the FAQs
14 Sue Trowbridge <trow@c TOP TEN LIST - Fri 9/8/95

You have been added to the TFTD-L list.

Summary of resource utilization
-------------------------------
 CPU time:        0.269 sec          Device I/O:     175
 Overhead CPU:    0.109 sec          Paging I/O:      10
 CPU model:        5990              DASD model:    3380
```

Select a message
1048
Read Electronic Mail

INST

15

Mailing Lists

❖ Subscribing to a Mailing List

This lesson will take you through the steps of subscribing to the TFTD-L mailing list. An Address Book entry will be created for the LISTSERV list manager followed by the SUBSCRIBE command sent to this entry's address.

Adding a LISTSERV Entry

1. Click **Internet**, then **Address Book.** Click **New Entry**.
2. Type **LISTSERV** in the Name box. Now press **TAB** or click the **Email Address** box.
3. Type **LISTSERV@TAMVM1.TAMU.EDU**. Press **TAB** or click the **Comments** box.
4. Type **Use for sending LISTSERV commands, not sending mail list messages**. (Or whatever denotes to you the difference.)

> ℹ *To send messages to a mailing list, create an entry for the list's address, then send the message using the entry after clicking the* **"Send Electronic Mail"** *icon. For example: the address for a mailing list relating to electronic music is EMUSIC-L@AMERICAN.EDU This address would be used in the Address Book.*

5. Click **OK**, then **Done**.

Subscribing to a Mailing List

6. Click the **"Send Electronic Mail"** icon on the Toolbar; or click **Internet**, then **Send Mail - Out**.
7. Click **LISTSERV** in the **...Or Choose Address From Address Book** box.
8. Click **Use**, then **OK**.
9. Leave the Subject: box empty. Press **ENTER** to move to the message area.
10. Type S**UBSCRIBE TFTD-L Your Name**.

> ℹ *Commands to LISTSERV are placed in the message area; the Subject: line is left blank. SUBSCRIBE is the command to add your name and address to the mailing list; TFTD-L is the list to subscribe to; and Your Name is the name you will be known by on the list. (Use your real name, not your Login Name or User Name.)*

11. Click the "**Send current message**" icon on the Mail window Toolbar.

After some time, two messages will be sent to you. The first message is an "Output of your job..." In other words, the output of the command(s) sent to LISTSERV. The second message is a notification that you are subscribed to the list, along with important information that should be saved. After reading the second message, click the **"Save current message"** icon to place it in the Saved Mail area. Some list messages request a reply to verify your mailing address.

Mailing Lists

Quick Reference Bar

To subscribe, send Email to LISTSERV@ TAMVM1.T AMU. EDU

Leave subject: line empty

Type Subscribe and the mailing list name in the message area

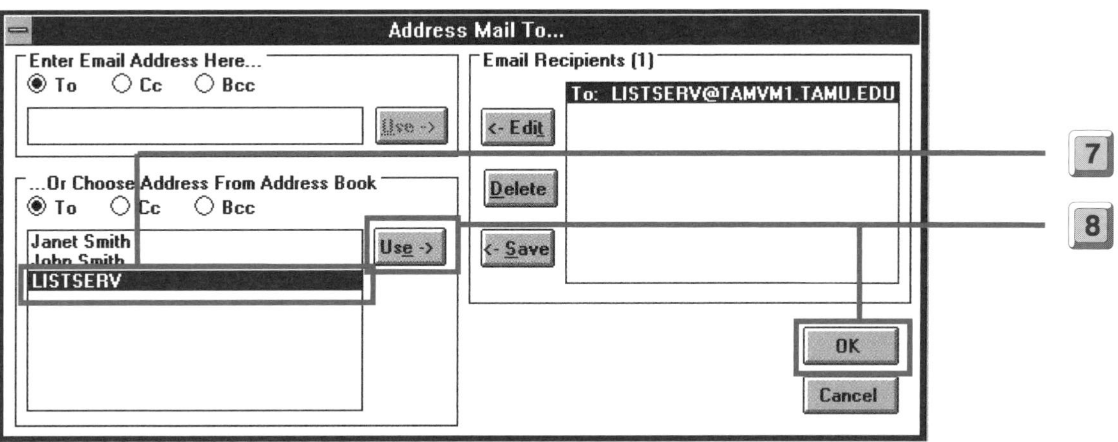

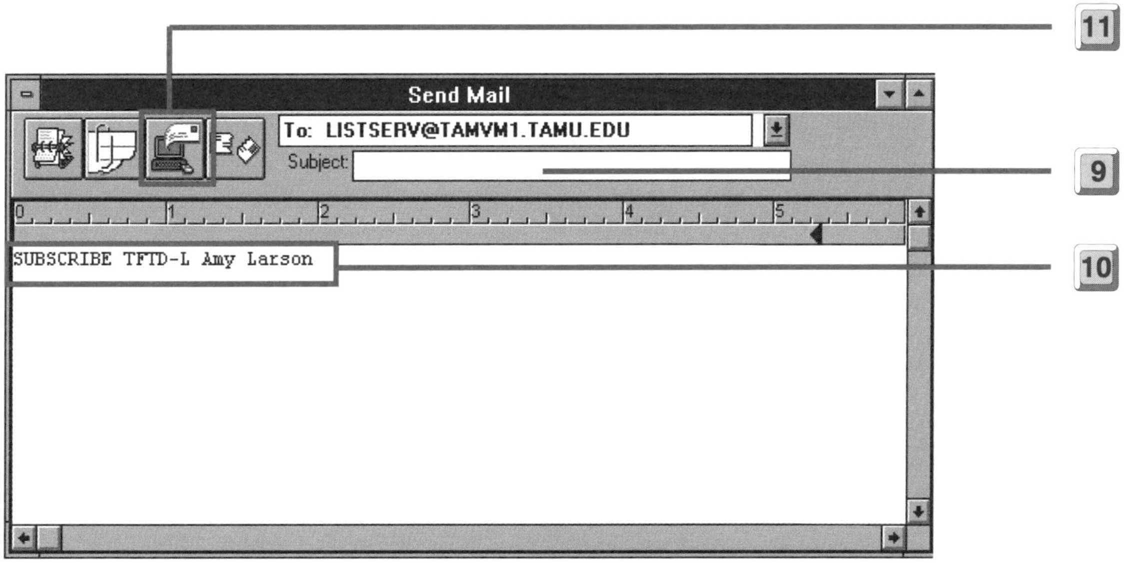

INST

16

Mailing Lists

❖ Signing Off a Mailing List

When you no longer want to be included on a mailing list, "signoff" the list. Signing off is as easy as subscribing. In this lesson you will learn how to send a message to LISTSERV, include the SIGNOFF command and indicate the appropriate mailing list.

Signing Off a Mailing List

1. Click the **"Send Electronic Mail"** icon on the Toolbar; or click **Internet**, then S**end Mail - Out**.

2. Click **LISTSERV** in the **...Or Choose Address From Address Book** box.

3. Click **Use**, then **OK**.

4. Leave the Subject: box empty. Press **ENTER** to move to the message area.

5. Type **SIGNOFF TFTD-L**

   SIGNOFF is the command to unsubscribe to a list and TFTD-L is the list to signoff from. Your Name is not required as it is when subscribing. If you want to stay subscribed to TFTD-L, cancel the message. Click the **control** *button, then* **close**. *Click* **Yes** *to cancel and skip step 6. Go to step 6 if you want to signoff.*

6. Click the "**Send current message"** icon on the Mail window Toolbar.

Mailing Lists

Quick Reference Bar

To Signoff, send Email to LISTSERV@TAMVM1.TAMV.EDU

Leave Subject: line empty

Type Signoff and the mailing list name in the message area

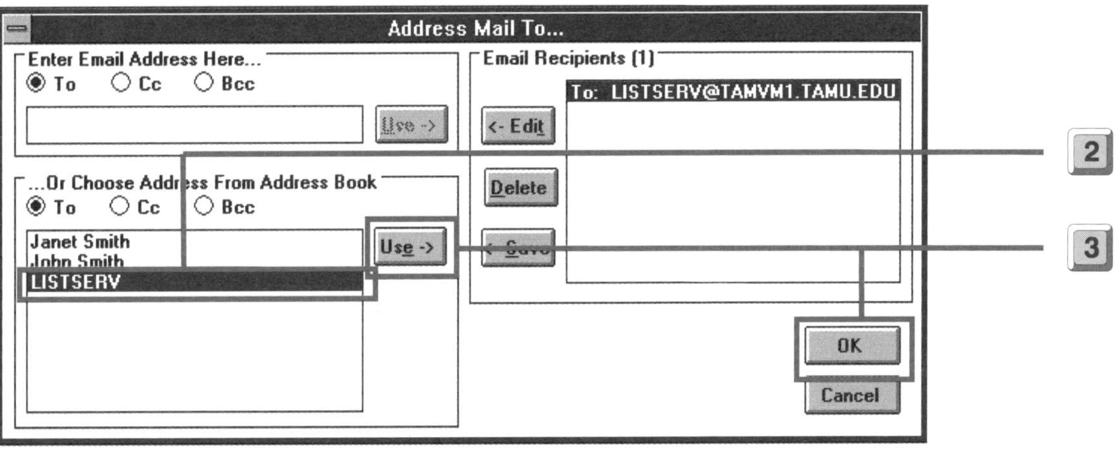

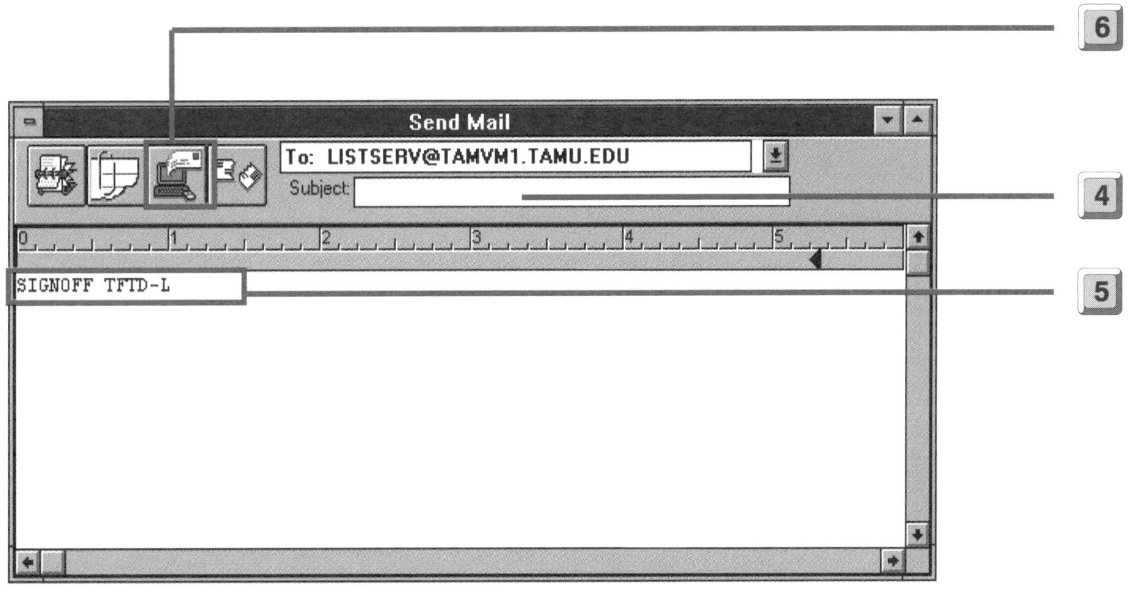

17 Mailing Lists

❖ Other LISTSERV Commands

LISTSERV supports other commands in addition to SUBSCRIBE and SIGNOFF. One of the most useful commands provides a list of available mailing lists to decide which ones are of interest. In this lesson you will learn how to receive Help and information on LISTSERV and how to register your name automatically when subscribing to a list.

1. Click the **"Send Electronic Mail"** icon on the Toolbar; or click **Internet**, then **Send Mail - Out**.
2. Click **LISTSERV** in the **...Or Choose Address From Address Book** box.
3. Click **Use**, then **OK**.
4. Leave the Subject: box empty. Press **ENTER** to move to the message area.
5. Type **LIST.**

List Command

LIST returns all mailing lists administered at **LISTSERV@TAMVM1.TAMU.EDU.** *To expand and include all list managers, use* **LIST GLOBAL**. *If a global list is more than you can digest, narrow down to a specific topic, use* **LIST GLOBAL TOPIC**. *For example: to get a global list relating to music, use* **LIST GLOBAL MUSIC**.

6. Click the **"Send current message"** icon on the Mail Window Toolbar.

Two messages will be sent to you. The first message is an "Output of your job..." reply. The second message is the result of your global search. To save the global search result to the local hard disk, double-click the message, then click the **"Save current message"** *icon. The message is saved in the Saved Mail area and to the local hard disk, \Netcom\Mail.*

Other LISTSERV commands

Following are other useful commands:

REGISTER Your Name - Registers the mailing list in your name automatically. Result: Your name does not need to be included in the SUBSCRIBE command.

HELP - Requests Help information available at the Host computer.

INFO - Returns a list of file names containing additional LISTSERV information, including less commonly used commands.

INFO Filename - Retrieves a file listed in the INFO command. Multiple commands can be sent in one message as long as they are entered in separate lines. For example: "REGISTER Tom Landon (line 1) INFO (line 2)" registers Tom Landon for any subsequent subscriptions and returns a list of files for further information on LISTSERV. Note that the Subject: line for these commands is also left blank.

Mailing Lists

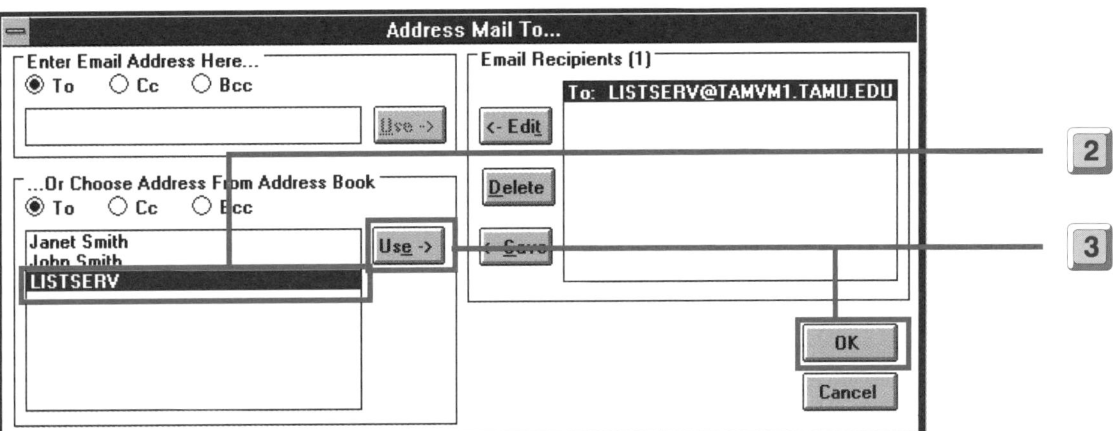

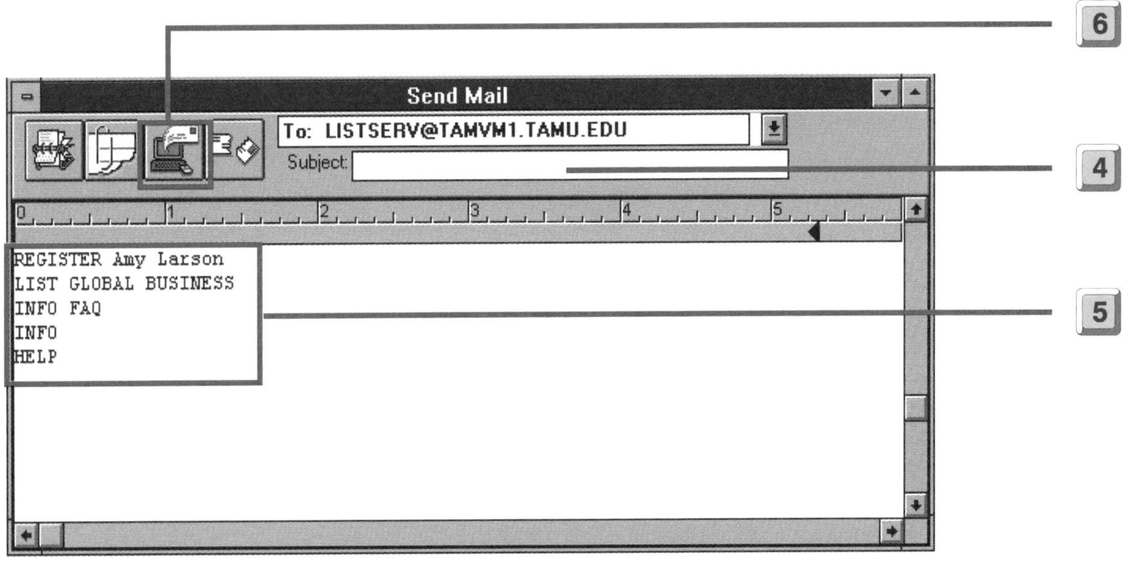

Quick Reference Bar

Use the LIST *command for a list of mailing lists*

Use the REGISTER *command to register your name*

Use the HELP *command for help with* LISTSERV

Use the INFO *command for a list of files*

18 World Wide Web

❖ World Wide Web Overview

Word Wide Web Formats

One of the newest Internet services, the World Wide Web allows businesses and hobbyists alike to store Internet documents in multiple formats for users to view. Formats include text, graphics, sound and even animation. A real estate company, for example, may use text to describe different properties and graphics for a visual affect. To take this one step further, animation may be used to simulate a "walk through" of a particular property, or an interactive area may be included where the user enters input from their keyboard. The location of these documents is said to be the developer's Web site, WWW site, Internet site, Web Page or ..., well you get the picture.

Hypermedia Links

"Hypermedia" is the term used for documents containing multiple formats. To move to different parts of the document, "links" or "hyperlinks" are built into the document and are accessed with the click of a mouse. If you have ever used a Windows Help program then you are familiar with links, the green underlined words that take you to a definition or a different topic. Links within a Web site are accessed the same way and may include links other than a green underline. For example: a graphic or a word within a heading may note the link.

A Web link may take you from a text portion of a document to additional and more detailed text or to a graphic picture within the document. Links can even be included to take the user to another Web site, physically stored on a remote computer somewhere else on the Internet network. Links within a document are intertwined, similar to a web, and sites are available throughout the world, hence the name "World Wide Web." For Web sites relating to the research of information, think of the links in the same manner as when retrieving information from a library. An index card may be used to get the main level of the topic with references to a more detailed subject matter.

HTML

To assure that each user sees the same information when "browsing" a Web site, a standard method for displaying the document was necessary. HTML (HyperText Markup Language) was the answer. HTML documents define the parts of the document but not the formatting itself. (Commands within the document may note the text as a heading for instance, but not the specifics of the text, like font size, bolding and italic characteristics.) Thus, documents can be viewed on numerous computers no matter what type of display they have. Oh, and one other requirement is needed to view Web sites, a Web Browser program, one that understands HTML commands. The browser uses the commands to create an accurate display on your monitor. No problem here, the NetCruiser program comes with a powerful Web Browser.

URLS

Accessing different items no matter what their type (text, graphic, sound and so forth) was another hurdle to overcome. The solution, a Uniform Resource Locator (URL) for each Web site. Take the **URL: http://www.eit.com/web/www.guide**. The first part in the URL notes the protocol to use for retrieving the item, http:, or HyperText Transfer Protocol for this example. (A protocol is a pre-defined method for accessing an Internet service.) The two forward slashes indicate that an Internet Host address or location follows. This can be either the document as in this example, or the actual address of the site. With the Internet's roots in the UNIX operating system, the path to the file uses forward slashes. Continuing with this example, www.eit.com is the Internet Host, /web indicates the directory, and www.guide is the file.

The above URL (Web site) provides an overview of the WWW, including information on HTML files and other areas that may be of interest. Feel free to "browse" this site for additional information you will learn in the following lesson. Note that NetCruiser supports protocols other than http; gopher:, ftp:, and telnet: protocols can all be accessed through the NetCruiser's Web Browser. You will learn about gopher, ftp and telnet in later lessons.

World Wide Web

Quick Reference Bar

Web sites may consist of text, graphics and sound

Click a link to move through a site

Enter the URL to locate a Site

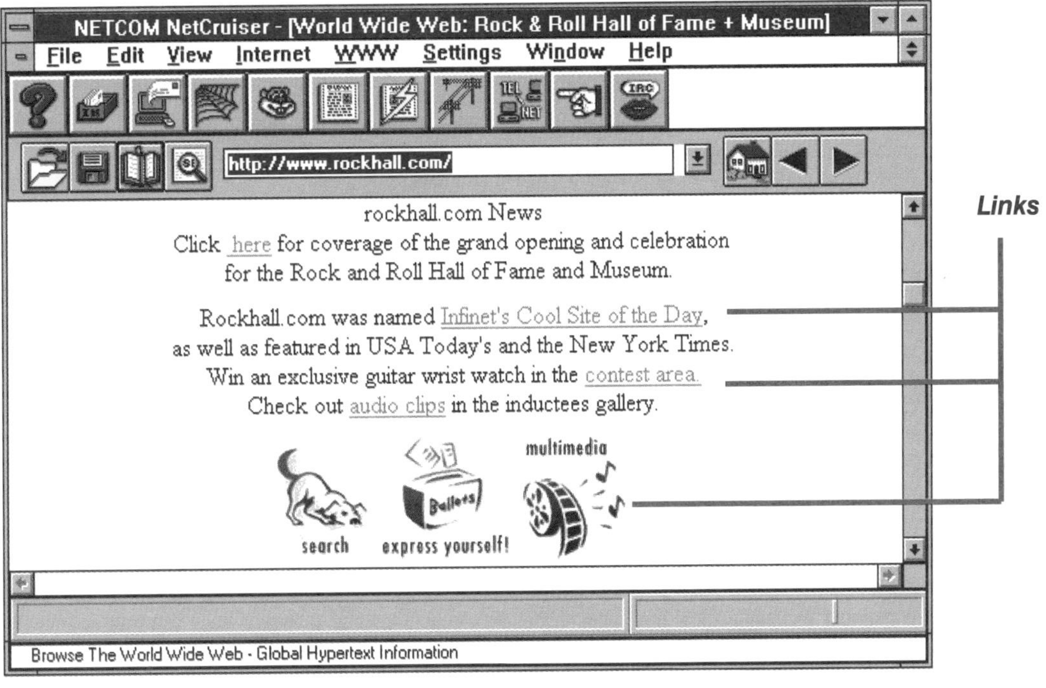

Links

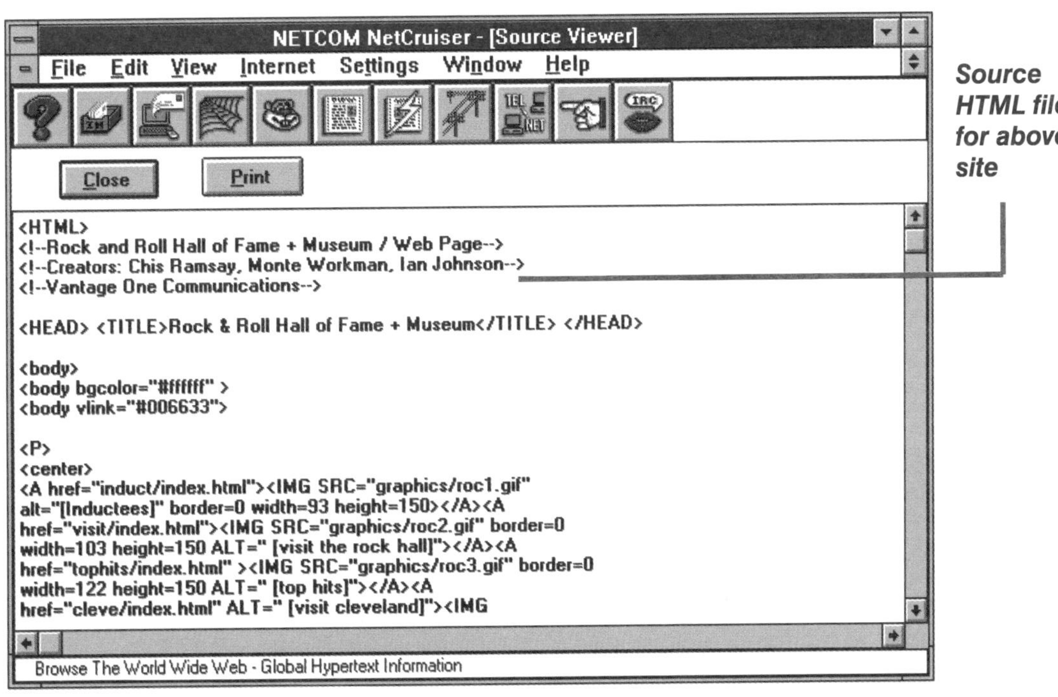

Source HTML file for above site

World Wide Web

❖ Exploring the NETCOM WWW Site

This lesson describes the steps to take for connecting to the NETCOM Web site, where links to other sites are available, as well as information relating to the NetCruiser program. You will also transfer to your computer the files required for working with file attachments included in Email and Usenet Newsgroups, as explained in lesson 8 of this training guide.

Browsing NETCOMM'S Web Site

1. Click the **"Browse The World Wide Web"** icon on the Toolbar; or click **Internet**, **World Wide Web - Browser**. Click the **NetCruiser** button towards the bottom of the screen.

2. Click the **Useful Windows Utilities** link. (You may need to click the **down arrow** in the scroll bar to see it.)

Downloading Files from a Site

3. Click **MPACK15D.ZIP**. Now wait for the file to be prepared for transfer. If an "Unknown type" window appears, leave the default radio button selected, then click **OK**.

4. Click **OK**. A "Save As" window appears with the file name: "mpack15d.zip" being sent to the \Netcom directory. Change the directory location for the file if desired or leave as is.

   The .ZIP extension in the file's name indicates it is in compressed form, and needs to be uncompressed before use. To uncompress, use PKUNZIP.EXE on the file after transfer. If you do not have PKUNZIP, transfer WINZIP56.EXE listed in the "Useful Windows Utilities" area. Afterward, run WINZIP56.EXE from the File, Run, Command Line: area in the Windows Program Manager. See any README files included for further information and license agreements.

5. Click **OK**. The file is transferred to the local computer.

6. Click the **down arrow** on the scroll bar to see other files. Click **WNCOD261.EXE**. Now wait for the file to be prepared for transfer.

   WNCOD261.EXE is a self-extracting file. Meaning: type **WNCOD261** at the DOS command prompt then press **ENTER**. Multiple files are extracted from within the file one of which is INSTALL.EXE. Run INSTALL.EXE from the File, Run, Command Line: area in the Windows Program Manager. The program will be installed. Use the Uuencode and Decode programs accordingly. Note the program requires payment to the author to receive its Help file.

7. Click **OK**. Another "Save As" window appears, with the file name: "wncod261.exe" being sent to the \Netcom directory. Change the directory location for the file if desired or leave as is.

8. Click **OK**. The file is transferred to the local computer.

Moving to a Previous Link

9. Click the **"Go to previous document"** icon to return to the starting point. Now click **V1.6 Frequently Asked Questions** for answers to common NetCruiser questions.

10. "Browse" the NETCOM area by clicking different links. Use the **"Go to previous document"** to return to the previous link. Now click "**other links to view**".

11. Close the Web window when done. Click its **Control** button, then **Close**.

World Wide Web

INST

19

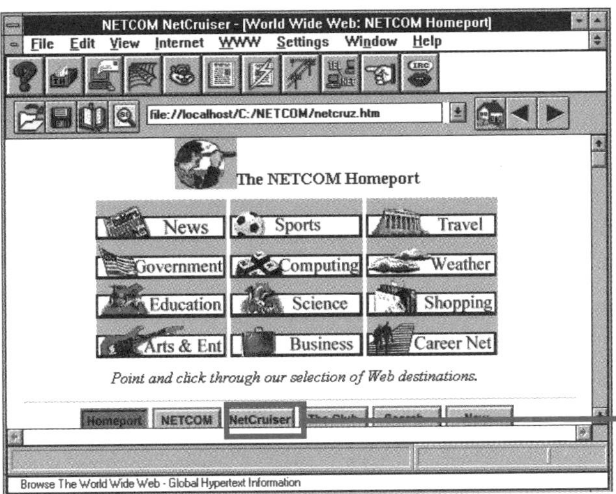

1

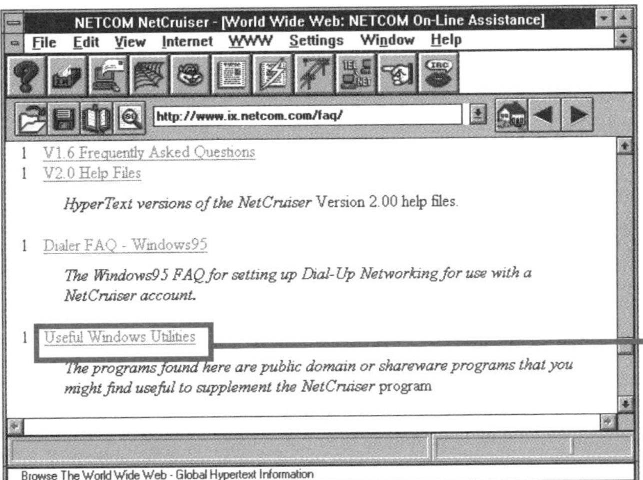

2

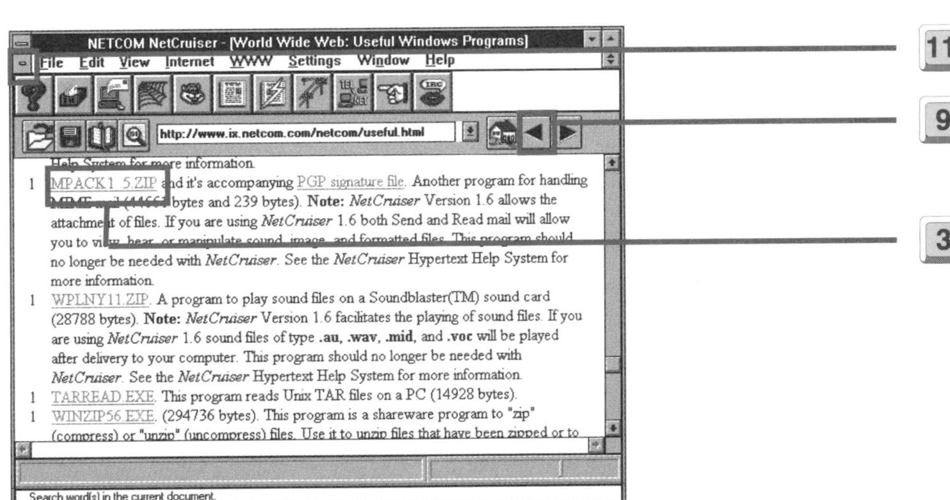

11

9

3

Quick Reference Bar

Click the "Browse The WWW" icon to browse a Site

Press CTRL+P to print a displayed page

Click View, Source file... to view HTML commands

Click close to return to previous view

Click "Go to home...", "Go to previous..." and "Go to next..." icons to move through a site

Press CTRL+F4 to close the Web window

INST

20

World Wide Web

❖ Finding and Book Marking a WWW Site

The number of Web sites on the Internet are many, with new ones added frequently. No doubt you will hear or read of a new site that's a "must see" and want to check it out for yourself. After making note of the site's address, connecting to it is simple, as explained in this lesson.

Entering a New Site

1. Click the **"Browse The World Wide Web"** icon on the Toolbar; or click **Internet**, **World Wide Web - Browser**.

2. Double-click **file://localhost/C:/NETCOM/netcruz.htm** in the WWW name box. The name is selected and can be replaced with the new Web site address. (The current name is not permanently removed.)

3. Type **http://www.msstate.edu/Movies** to enter the new site address. (Notice the upper case "M" in Movies. Always enter the address exactly as it appears.)

4. Press **ENTER**. NetCruiser connects to the remote site and displays its opening screen. (By the way, this is a movie database site at Mississippi State University.)

Book Marking a Site

5. Book mark the site. Click the **"Open the book mark file"** icon. The name: of the site is filled in along with its URL:. Click **Add**.

Once an area is book marked, you can "jump" to this area without having to enter its address. Just click the **"Open the book mark file"** *icon after the opening screen (step 1). Click the* **book mark**, *then* **Jump**. *Any area of the site can be marked, not just the opening screen. Move to the appropriate area first and then use the "Open the book mark file" icon.*

Returning to a Home Page

6. Click **Close**. Click the **"Go to home page"** icon on the Toolbar.

7. Return to the book marked site. Click the **"Open the book mark file"** icon.

8. Click **"Main Page: The Internet Movie Database..."**. Click **Jump**.

9. Browse the page. Close the Web window when done. Click the **Control** button, then **Close**.

You can also book mark a site by entering the site's Name: and URL: in the "book mark" area. From the opening "Browse The World Wide Web" screen (step 1), click the **"Open the book mark file"** *icon, then replace the current Name: and URL: with the desired site's information (the original Name: and URL: are not permanently removed). Now click* **Add**.

Displaying the graphics within a site can be turned off to allow a faster "screen draw" time. You may want to do this when "browsing" for only the text contents of different sites. Click **Settings**, **WWW Options**, *then* **View**. *Click the* **X** *in the* **"Display in line images"** *area. Click again to turn back on. You can also change the font type and size from this area. Click on* **Fonts**.

World Wide Web

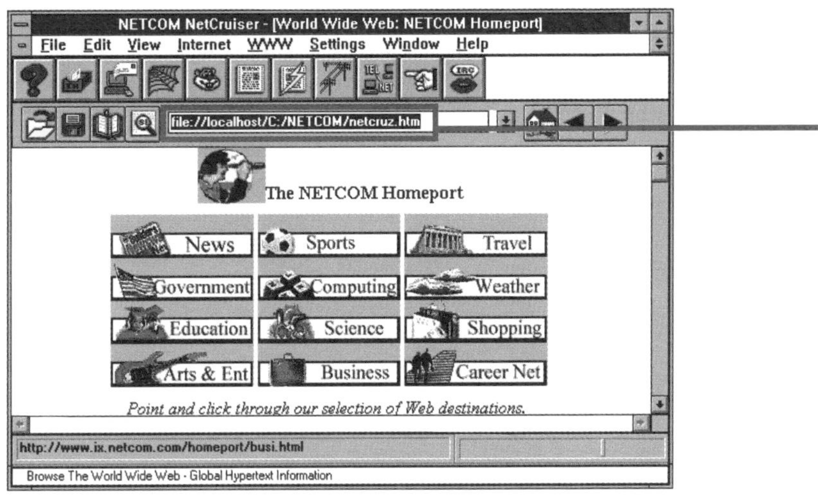

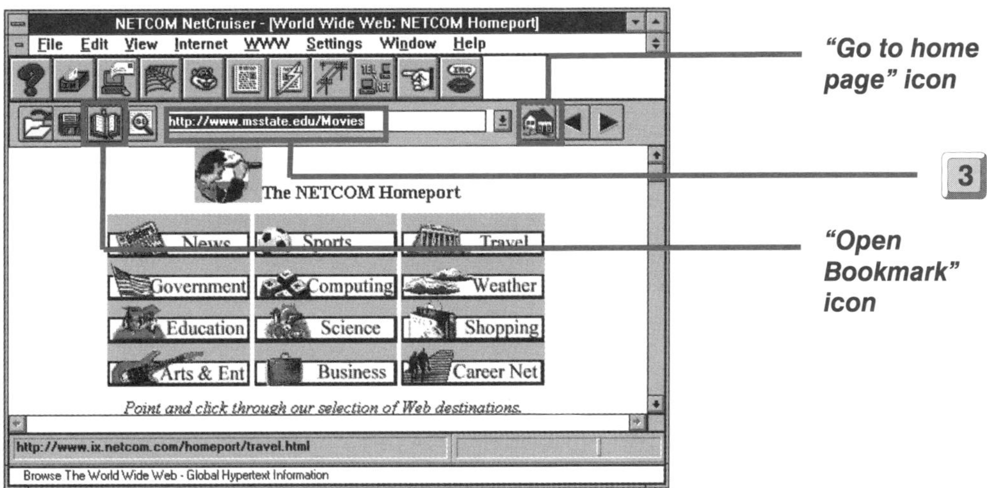

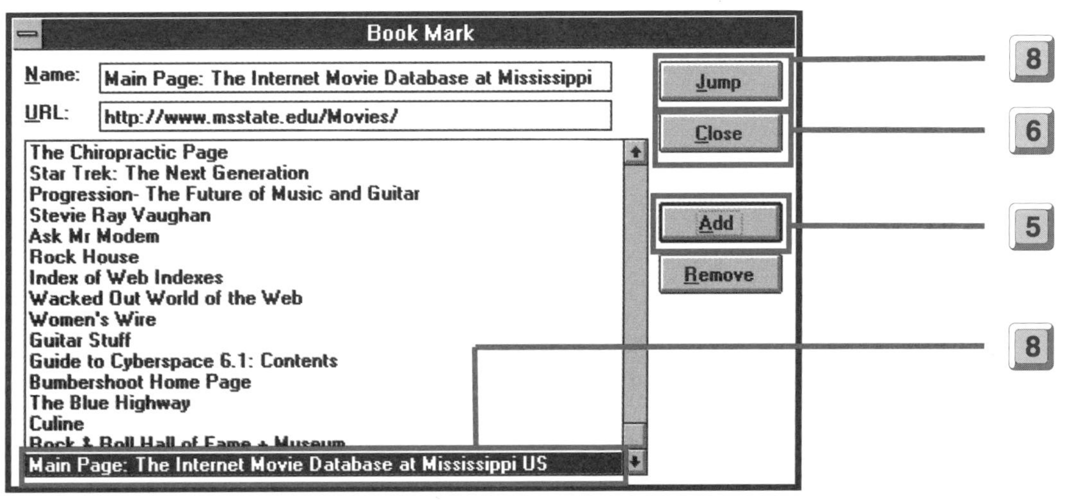

Click "Open the book mark file" to bookmark a Site

Click "Jump" to move to a book marked Site

Click "Remove" to delete a book marked Site

File Transfer Protocol (FTP)

❖ FTP Overview

From its inception, the Internet was designed to share information in the form of electronic files. To accomplish this task a protocol was developed, the File Transfer Protocol, or FTP. (A protocol is a standard way of regulating data transmission between computers.) A user connects to a server computer, initiates the FTP, and sends or receives a file or group of files. Unlike Email or UseNet file attachments, FTP directly supports ASCII and Binary files without any conversion required. You do however need to tell the FTP server which type of file is being transferred.

Transferring Files

The FTP is a program that runs from the server (remote), and is initiated from a client (local) FTP program, like the one within NetCruiser. Receiving a file is called a "download" while sending a file is called an "upload." When transferring files the message "Too many connections, try again later..." (or something similar) may be received. In this case, do try later, in off-peak hours if possible. Remember that many users can connect to the same server computer.

Most of your Internet FTP connections will involve downloading files to your local computer. Uploading files may be required if you are involved with the development of a program, utility, etc. and need to send updates to the server.

Anonymous FTP's

Some FTP servers are for public use, anyone can connect to them and download or upload files. A server falling into this category is an "Anonymous FTP." Other servers are private and require an account to access the server: A name and password are required for entrance. For anonymous FTPs, the name "anonymous" and a password of "guest," "Your Name," or the user's Internet address may be used depending on the server.

How file names appear on a server depends on the type of system in use. A UNIX system may have file names in upper or lower case and be of any length. A VMS system (from Digital Equipment Corporation) will have file names only in upper case. PC and Macintosh display files in their standard format.

Index Files

Most servers (especially large archive sites) will have an index of the available files along with a description. Look for a file called "Index" (in upper or lower case), or README. For questions about the FTP server or the files it contains, sending mail to the server's "postmaster" may get the answer. Send mail to "postmaster" followed by the server's address, postmaster@servers.address.com for example. Some servers may have a different person to contact. In this case the name may appear when first connecting to the server or be contained within a README file.

File Transfer Protocol (FTP)

Quick Reference Bar

FTP is a protocol for sending and receiving files

Binary files can be transferred without conversion

Selecting a "Binary" format is fine for most files

See README and Index files for information on files and FTP servers

FTP Server

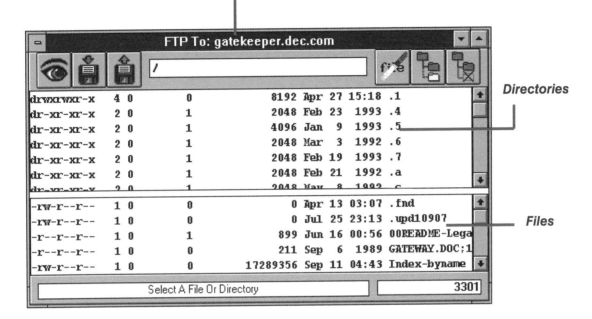

FTP To: gatekeeper.dec.com

/

Directories

```
drwxrwxr-x  4 0   0      8192 Apr 27 15:18 .1
dr-xr-xr-x  2 0   1      2048 Feb 23  1993 .4
dr-xr-xr-x  2 0   1      4096 Jan  9  1993 .5
dr-xr-xr-x  2 0   1      2048 Mar  3  1992 .6
dr-xr-xr-x  2 0   1      2048 Feb 19  1993 .7
dr-xr-xr-x  2 0   1      2048 Feb 21  1992 .a
```

Files

```
-rw-r--r--  1 0   0         0 Apr 13 03:07 .fnd
-rw-r--r--  1 0   0         0 Jul 25 23:13 .upd10907
-r--r--r--  1 0   1       899 Jun 16 00:56 00README-Lega
-r--r--r--  1 0   0       211 Sep  6  1989 GATEWAY.DOC;1
-rw-r--r--  1 0   0  17289356 Sep 11 04:43 Index-byname
```

Select A File Or Directory | 3301

File Format Selection

FTP To: gatekeeper.dec.com

Download "README.ftp" as:

Binary File

ASCII Text

Cancel

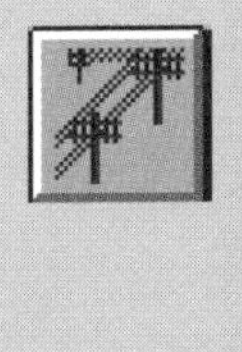

INST

22 File Transfer Protocol (FTP)

❖ Connecting to an FTP Server

This lesson describes the steps for connecting to an FTP server. You will also learn how to "browse" a server and download its available files.

Selecting an FTP Server

1 Click the **"FTP File Transfer"** icon on the Toolbar; or click **Internet**, **FTP Download**.

The opening screen displays the "FTP Site: Chooser" map, containing sites throughout the US. You can click one of the states, then the **drop-down** arrow to see the servers in that area. This is useful if you are familiar with these servers. If you are not familiar with them manually type in a known server's address as in step 2. This method will probably be used most often as you tour the Internet and discover FTP sites you'd like to visit.

2 Type **ftp.cica.indiana.edu** then press **ENTER**. Wait for the connection to this server which is the "Center for Innovative Computer Applications."

Connecting to an FTP Server

3 An "FTP To: ..." window appears with the Username: Anonymous and the Password: xxxxxxxx.ix.netcom.com. Click **OK**. A "Connecting ..." message appears at the bottom of the screen. Wait for the connection.

4 An "... FTP Message" window appears with information regarding the server. Read the message (Yes it's small type. No way to change this with NetCruiser.) Click the window's **Control** button, then **Close**.

Viewing Files on an FTP Server

5 A window appears listing the directories and files. If desired, increase its size. Click the **up arrow** at the top right of the window.

The window contains a top and a bottom pane. Directories show in the top pane while files within the current directory show in the bottom pane. Double-click a directory to open it and display its files in the bottom pane.

6 Double-click the **"pub"** directory, then **"pc"** in the top pane. (Click the **down arrow** on the vertical scroll bar if "pc" does not show.)

7 Double-click the **"win3"** directory in the top pane. (Click the **down arrow** on the vertical scroll bar if "win3" does not show.) Another "... FTP Message" window may appear. Read the message then close the window as in step 4.

From here you see the directories relating to Windows ver. 3, such as "desktop", "fonts", "games", etc. Double-click a directory to see its available files. To select a file for download, click the file in the bottom pane. To select more than one, press and hold down the **CTRL** key and click each file. Afterward, click the **"Download a file from the remote computer"** icon. When sending a file, click the **"Upload a file to the remote computer"** icon.

When downloading files, a message appears asking if the file is ASCII or Binary. Select accordingly. When in doubt, select Binary. This method is fine for most types of files, even ASCII.

8 Browse through the directories and download files if you like. Close the FTP window.

File Transfer Protocol (FTP)

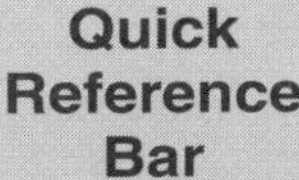

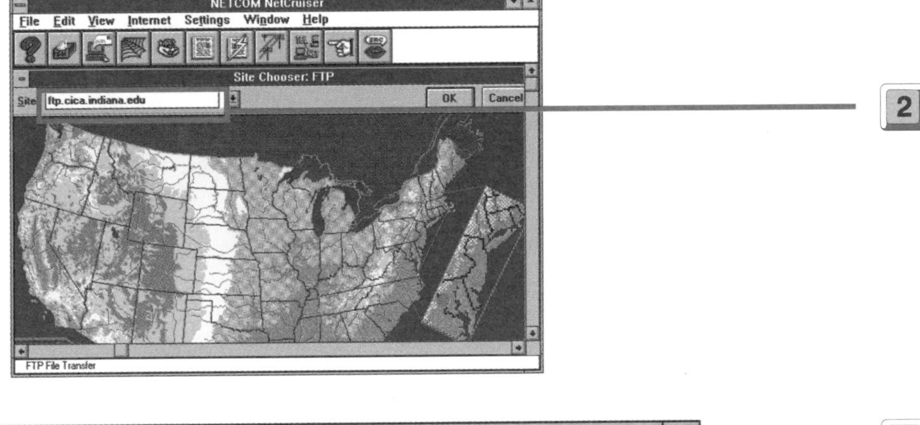

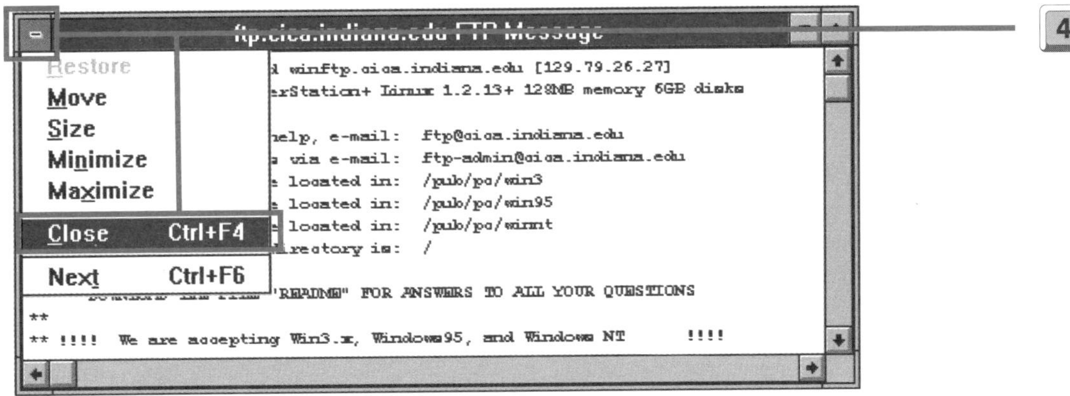

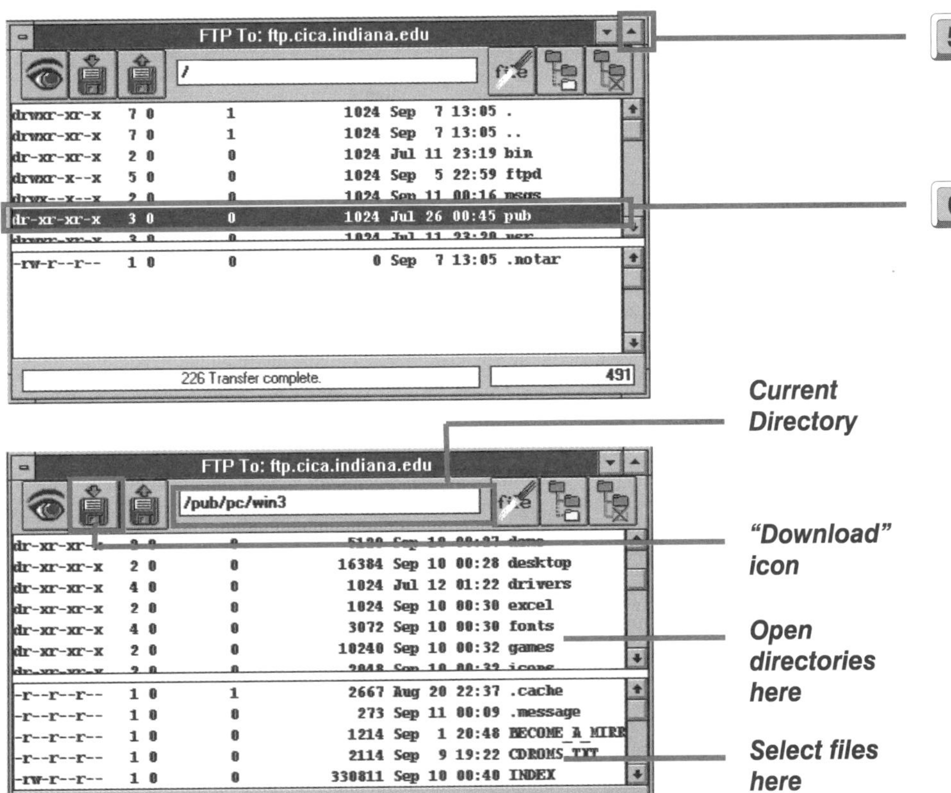

Click the "FTP File Transfer" icon to connect to a server

Double-click Directory in the top pane to open directions

Click Files in bottom pane to download files

Press CTRL+F4 to close a FTP window

Click the "Down Load..." icon to receive a file

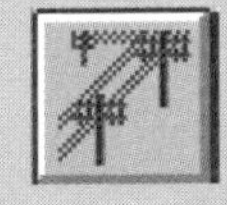

23 Gopher

❖ Gopher Overview

Background

And now an introduction to the most popular rodent in Cyberspace, Gopher. An odd name for sure in such a high-tech environment, but maybe not so when its roots are know. Gopher was developed at the University of Minnesota and accordingly named for its mascot, the gopher. A tool for browsing and retrieving files, the name is also derived from the old adage of what it does, it "goes fer this, and goes fer that."

Browsing a Gopher Server

Unlike a direct FTP connection, Gopher provides a simpler method of browsing the Internet for information. Locating information through a Gopher server is easier because its menus appear in a structured mode similar to a book's table of contents. Gopher menus also include a description along with the name of a particular file to give you an idea of whether or not you'd like to transfer the file to your computer. Most Gopher servers contain links to other sites, so once connected other resources are available.

Gopher is a protocol run from a server (remote) computer. To use the protocol a Gopher client is run from the local computer and a connection is made to a server. A client is already available to you with the NetCruiser program. Client software can connect to a Gopher server or many FTP sites directly. In the following lesson you will connect to an FTP site by using the Gopher client and choose the same FTP server as in the previous lesson. How Gopher displays the items differently will be seen.

Gopher's Efficiency

Even with Gopher's ease of use, there is another reason to use it over other services. Gopher is a "real time" protocol. When a Gopher client makes a request from the server the data is sent and the connection closes in real time. Other protocols (FTP for instance) keep the port on the server tied up preventing others from connecting. Using Gopher is a more efficient use of Internet resources.

Gopher Items

Items within a Gopher menu are denoted by a small icon to represent the item's type. A Yellow icon notes a directory. Double-click the directory and other files appear. (A connection may also be made to another server if that's where those files reside.) A small White icon notes a text file. A small Green icon notes a binary file.

23 Gopher

Quick Reference Bar

Gopher is a protocol for browsing information

Gopher displays items in structured menus

Gopher is a "Real Time" protocol

Press CTRL+F4 to close a Gopher window

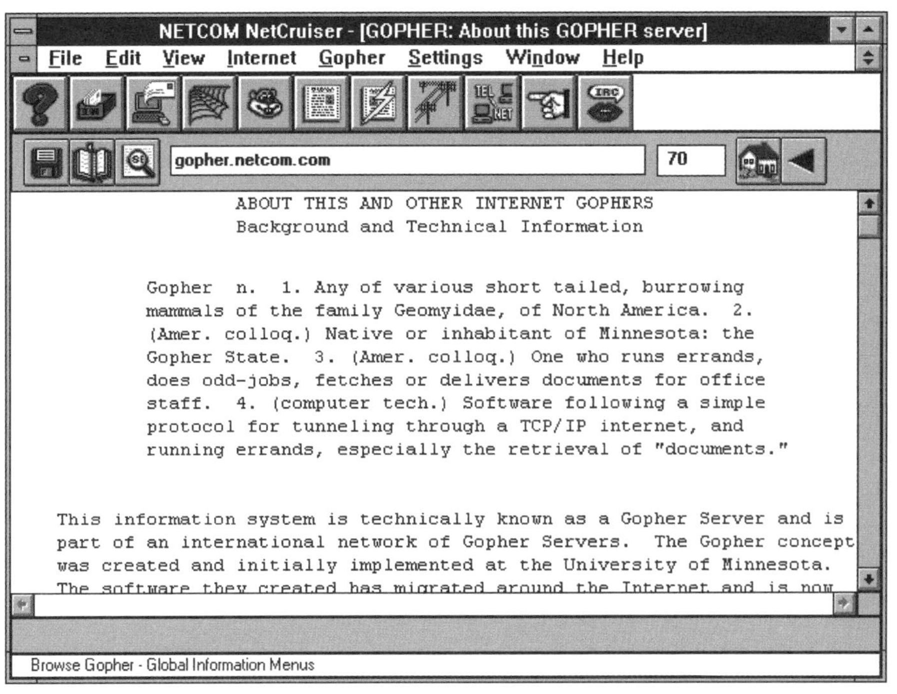

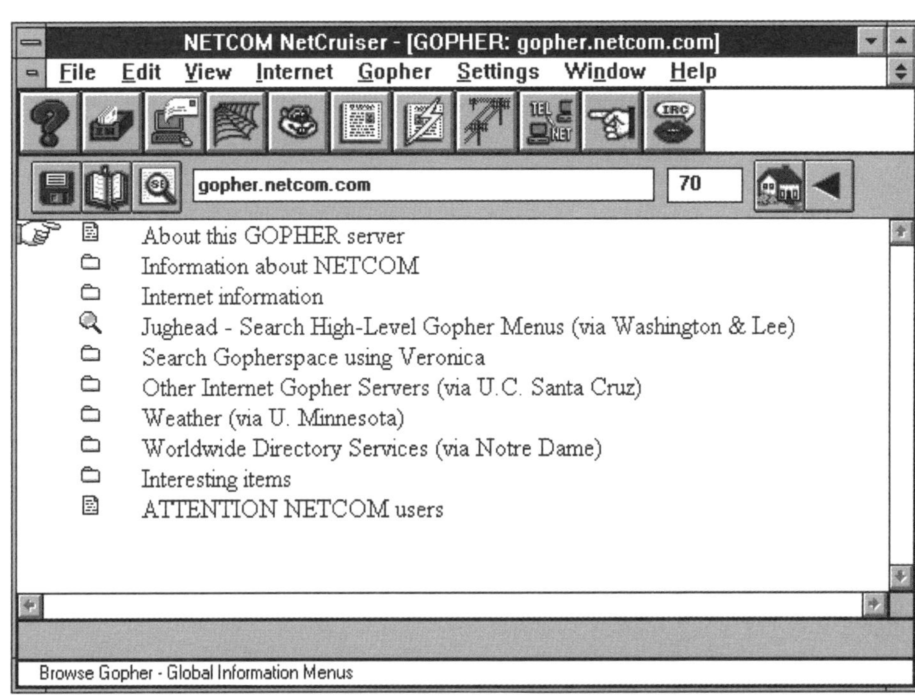

Gopher

❖ Browsing and Retrieving Files with Gopher

You will now browse the files available on the FTP server accessed in lesson 21, using the Gopher protocol in place of FTP.

Selecting a Gopher Server

1. Click the **"Browse Gopher - Global Information Menus"** icon on the Toolbar; or click **Internet, Gopher - Browser**.

   The opening screen displays the "Gopher Site: Chooser" map containing sites throughout the US. You can click one of the states, then the **drop-down** arrow to see the servers in that area. This is useful if you are familiar with these servers. If you are not familiar with them, manually type in a known server's address as in step 2. This method will probably be used most often as you tour the Internet and discover Gopher sites you'd like to visit.

2. Double-click **gopher.netcom.com** in the Site: box. The name is selected and can be replaced with the new site address. (The current name is not permanently removed.)

Connecting to a Gopher Server

3. Type **ftp.cica.indiana.edu** then press **ENTER**. Wait for the connection to this server which is the "Center for Innovative Computer Applications."

4. Double-click the **PC and CICA Windows Files** directory.

5. Double-click the **CICA Windows Files** directory.

> *The same directories appear as when accessing the server through FTP, "Desktop", "Fonts" and "Games", etc., except the menu is more easily understood and convenient to move through. Double-click a directory (a yellow icon) to open it and view its contents.*

> *To download a text file (White icon), double-click the file. The file's contents appear in the window. Click the* **"Save the current document to disk"** *icon; or click* **File**, **Save**; *or press* **CTRL+S**. *A "Save As" window appears. Open a different directory if you like or leave as is. Click* **OK**.

Downloading Files

To download a binary file (Green icon), double-click the file. A "Save As" window appears. Open a different directory if you like or leave as is. Click **OK**.

Book Marking a Location

To "book mark" the location for a future connection, click the **"Open book mark file"** icon; or click **Gopher**, **Book Mark**. The Name: and URL: are filled in. Click **Add**, then **Close**. Any area can be marked. Move to the desired area first. Note that to "Jump" to a book mark, a Gopher connection must be made. Open Gopher (step 1) then connect to the default server, gopher.netcom.com. Click **OK** from this screen. Now click the **"Open book mark file"** icon.

6. Browse through the directories and download files if you like. Close the Gopher window when done. Click its **Control** button, then **Close**.

Gopher

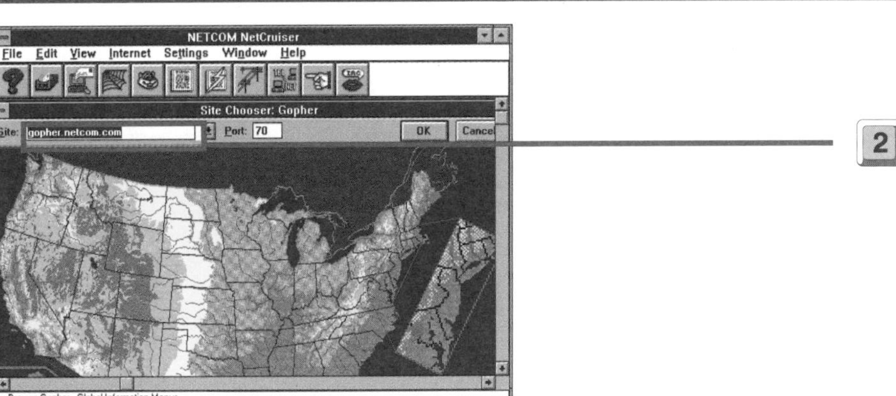

2

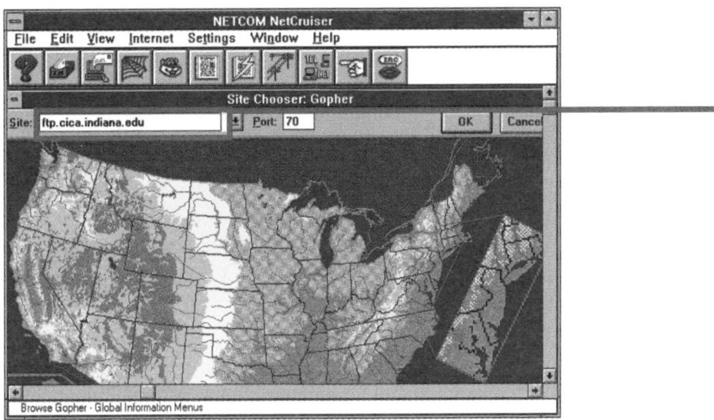

3

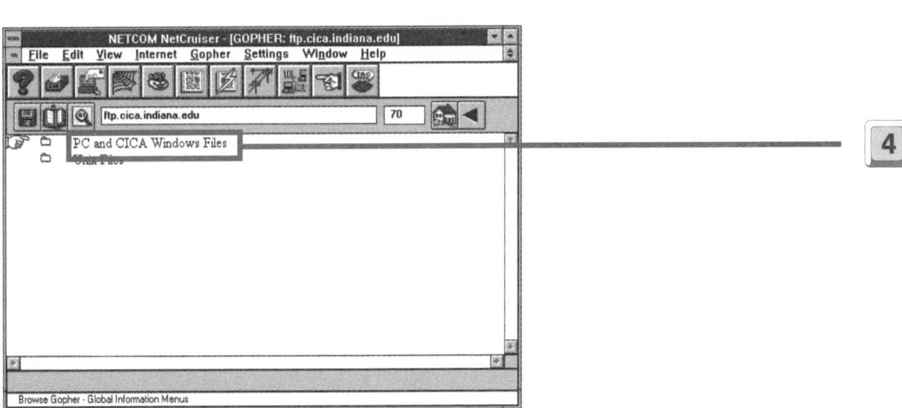

4

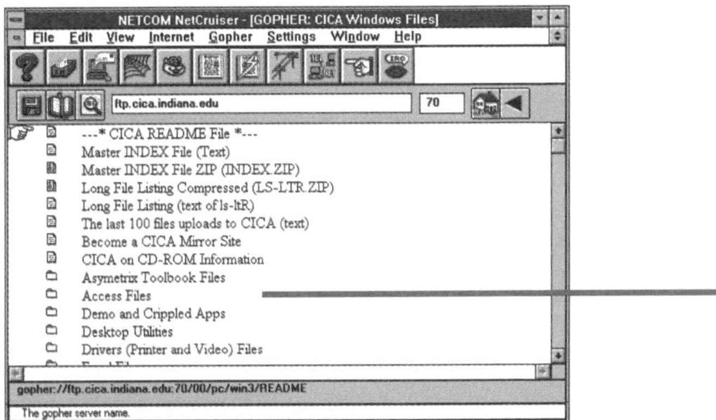

Directories

Quick Reference Bar

Click the "Browse Gopher..." icon to connect to a server

Click File, Play Sound File *to listen to an audio file*

Click File, View Graphics File *to see a graphic file*

Click File, View Text File *to see a text file*

Press CTRL+F4 *to close a Gopher window*

Gopher

 Veronica

With the number of resources on the Internet being close to infinite, a way of searching for them was needed. Veronica was one solution as described in this lesson.

Accessing Veronica

 Veronica is a service accessed through a Gopher client and server. No Veronica "client" exists per say, such as with Gopher, FTP and WWW. You can use the Gopher client provided with NetCruiser to connect to a Gopher server providing Veronica service and perform a search.

File Indexes

 Veronica keeps an index of files available on Gopher servers. By keeping an index users can search for specific subjects of interest.

Veronica Menus

 Veronica menus may display multiple servers that can be used for searching. Theoretically it shouldn't matter which server you access—for the most part they all contain the same index of files. Keep in mind however that network traffic will be different between servers and their index updates will vary. Thus, trying a different server or connecting during "off peak" hours may be needed in some instances.

Title Searches

 Item "Titles" of the file names are searched as they appear on the Gopher server.

 Veronica stands for: Very Easy Rodent-Oriented Net-wide Index to Computerized Archives. An obvious "pun" on the term Gopher, developers of Internet services have kept their sense of humor. The name was also a spin off of the service used for searching files of FTP sites, Archie. Presently, Archie is limited in its search function as it looks for file names only. It does not search their titles.

Gopher

INST

25

Quick Reference Bar

Veronica is a service, not a "Client" program

Access Veronica through a Gopher client and server

Veronica menus display servers to search

Veronica searches item "Titles"

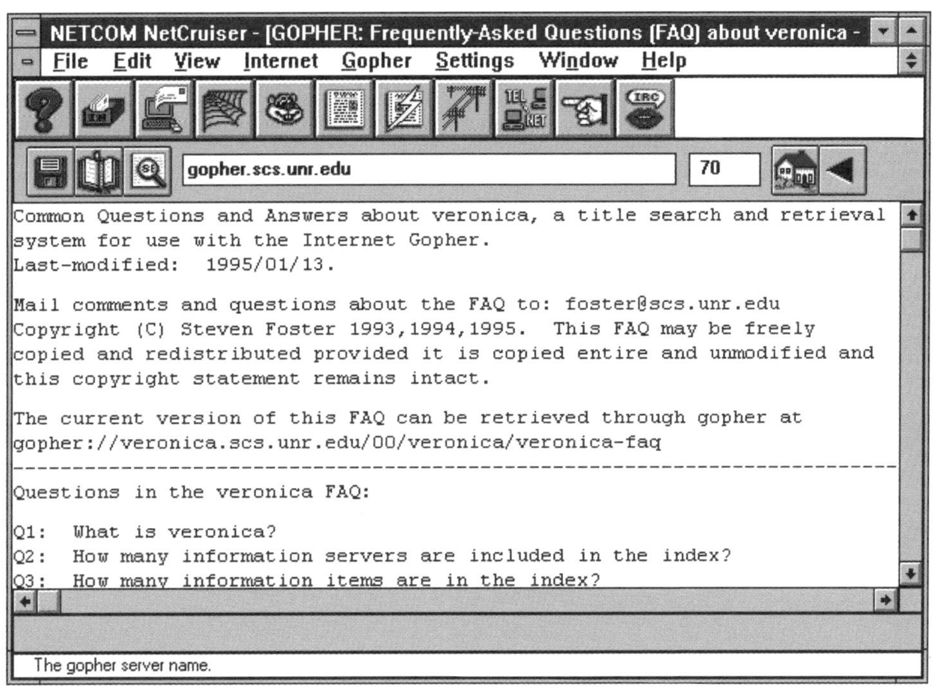

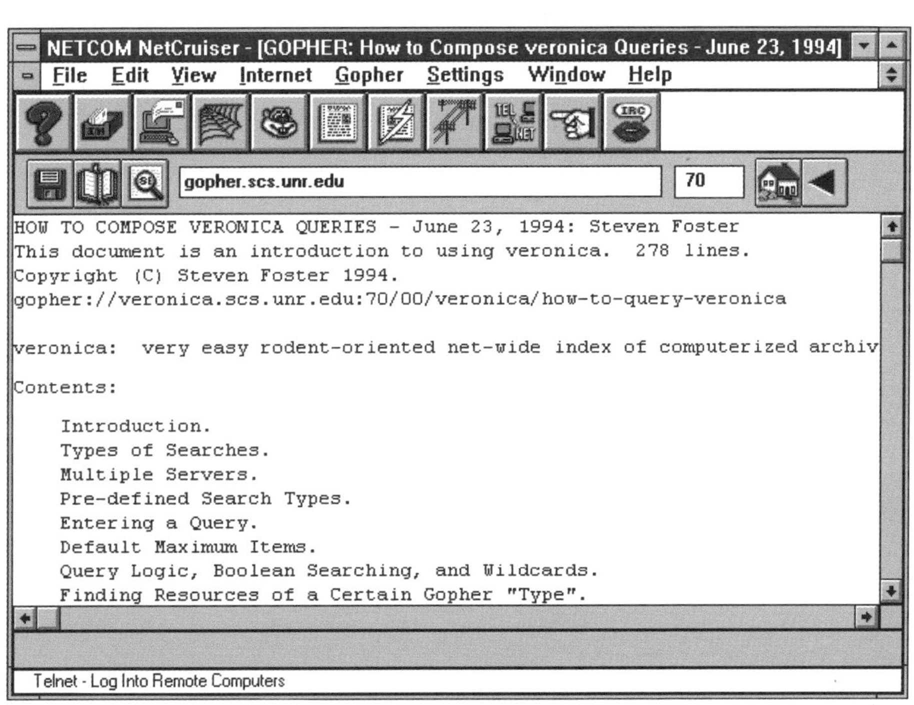

Gopher

❖ Using Veronica to Search for Files

You will now connect to a Gopher server offering Veronica and search for files. The GOPHER.NETCOM.COM server will be used.

Connecting to a Gopher Server

1 Click the **"Browse Gopher - Global Information Menus"** icon on the Toolbar; or click **Internet**, **Gopher - Browser**.

2 Click **OK**. A connection is made to the gopher.netcom.com server. Increase the window size if you like by clicking the **up arrow** at the top right of the Gopher window.

Accessing Veronica

3 Double-click the **"Search Gopherspace using Veronica"** item. A list of servers offering Veronica appears in the Gopher menu.

> *You may want to "book mark" this area to return later and search for files. To book mark, click the* **"Open book mark file"** *icon. The Name: and URL: are filled in. Click* **Add**, *then* **Close**. *To return to the area, run Gopher and connect to any Site (steps 1 and 2), then click the* **"book mark"** *icon, the* **Veronica** *mark, then* **OK**.

Entering Search Criteria

4 Double-click one of the servers. A message "Please enter search string:" appears.

5 Type a word or group of words to search for in the file name titles.

> *Veronica supports the Boolean operations of AND, NOT and OR. When appropriate, use them to narrow down the search. Also supported is the DOS wildcard, * (an asterisk), but only at the end of words.*

Beginning a Search

6 Click **OK** to begin the search.

> *If any matches are found, a list of items appears with links to the Gopher server containing the files. Click the items to connect to that server. You can then download and view files etc. through the same process as when connecting directly to a Gopher server, as in lesson 23.*

> *For further information on Veronica, download the file "Frequently-Asked Questions (FAQ) about Veronica - Date" and "How to Compose Veronica Queries - Date" from the opening Veronica screen (step 3).*

7 Browse for files of interest. Close the Gopher window when done. Click its **Control** button, then **Close**.

Gopher

Quick Reference Bar

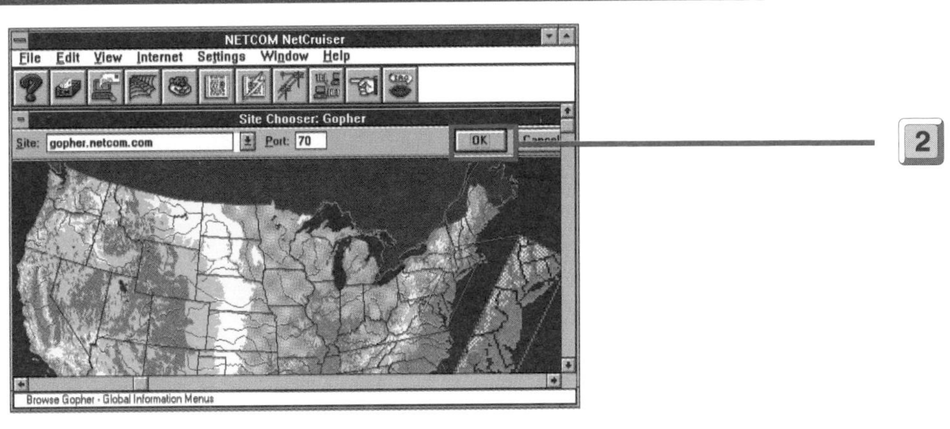

2

Double-click "Search Gopher-space..." to access Veronica

Double-click a server to enter a search string

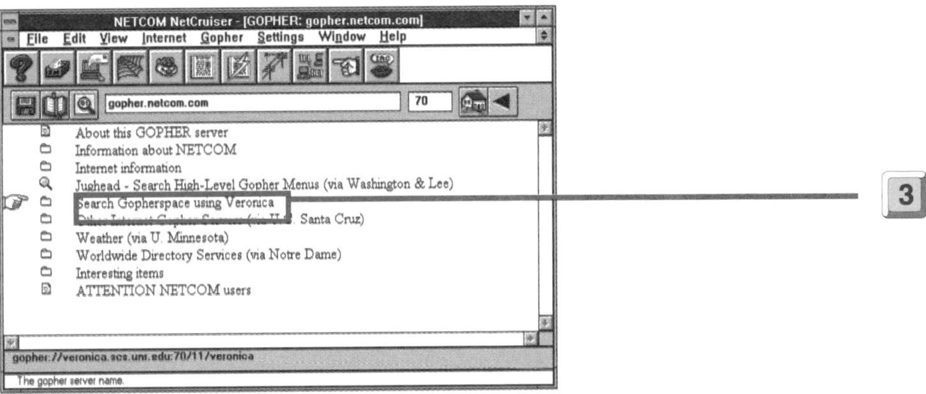

3

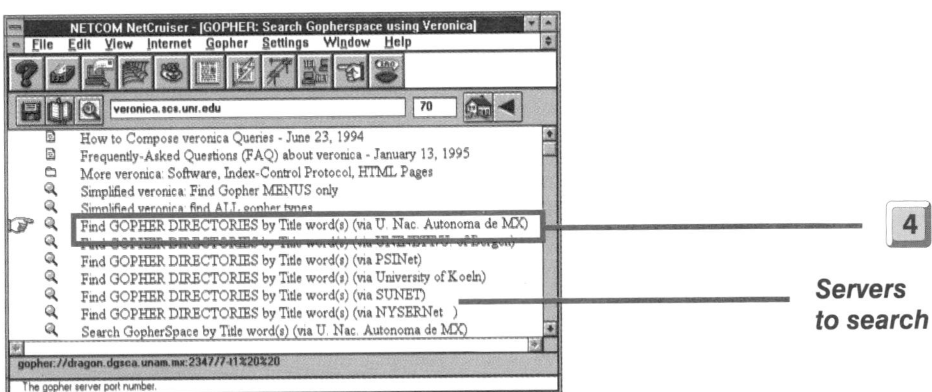

4

Servers to search

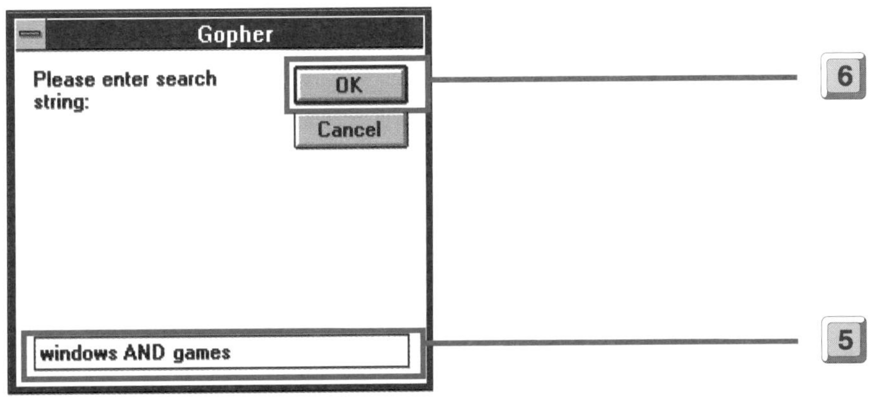

6

5

Telnet

❖ Understanding Telnet

Telnet allows you to connect to a remote computer and "take over". By taking over, the keystrokes entered from your local keyboard are actually executed on the remote. Following are some of the details and limitations pertaining to Telnet.

Protocol

1. Telnet is a protocol. A set of instructions is used to determine how information is shared. The Telnet protocol is used to transfer commands from the local keyboard (the one you are working on) to the remote computer (the one you are connected to).

2. In the early computing days, large computers were used to process information. Data was entered through terminal machines and processed on the larger ones. Terminals did not have Central Processing Units as do most of today's computers. Telnet operates similarly.

Terminals

3. Standard types of terminals were developed to assure connectivity with the larger computers. Digital Equipment Corporation (DEC) provided many of these terminals, noted as the DEC VT100 and VT102 (a slight variation), and the VT 52 and VT220 series.

4. Other types of terminals include ANSI and TTY. ANSI terminals can display some text in color and TTY terminals are the most basic in design, usually depending on the remote computer to determine how information is displayed on the screen. TTY is a teletype-style terminal similar to the ones used in older newsrooms.

Terminal Emulators

5. Most computers on the Internet support VT100 for compatibility. To connect with these computers a terminal program is used to emulate the VT100 terminal on the local computer. (Today's terminals are more sophisticated than the VT100. The emulation program is needed to "dumb down" the local terminal.)

6. NetCruiser provides this emulation with its Telnet client. It supports: Generic/TTY and VT100/ANSI emulation. VT100/ANSI is set as the default.

Telnet Host Connection

7. Some remote computers require TN3270 emulation. If you get the message "Connection closed by foreign host," or "VM or MVS" in the welcome screen you will need to "Telnet" to a public host offering a TN3270 emulator. Some host computers require a Name, Address, Email Address and (or) a credit card number before connecting. Use your best judgment before accessing these hosts.

8. If you receive a constant "Trying..." message when connecting but nothing else, the remote computer may be extremely busy or down for some reason. Break out of the connection by pressing **CTRL+]** or close the Telnet window.

9. Once a Telnet connection is made its execution is done in the background. You may even forget its there. Even so, remember that the connection may be provided through multiple computers and take some time to process commands. When Internet activity is high you may notice a sluggish reaction. This is normal and does not necessarily mean something is wrong.

10. If you cannot connect to a remote computer through its host name, try its numeric address. Host names are converted to their numeric values through Name Server computers throughout the Internet. The conversion will not occur if a server goes down, but you can still connect using its numeric address.

Telnet

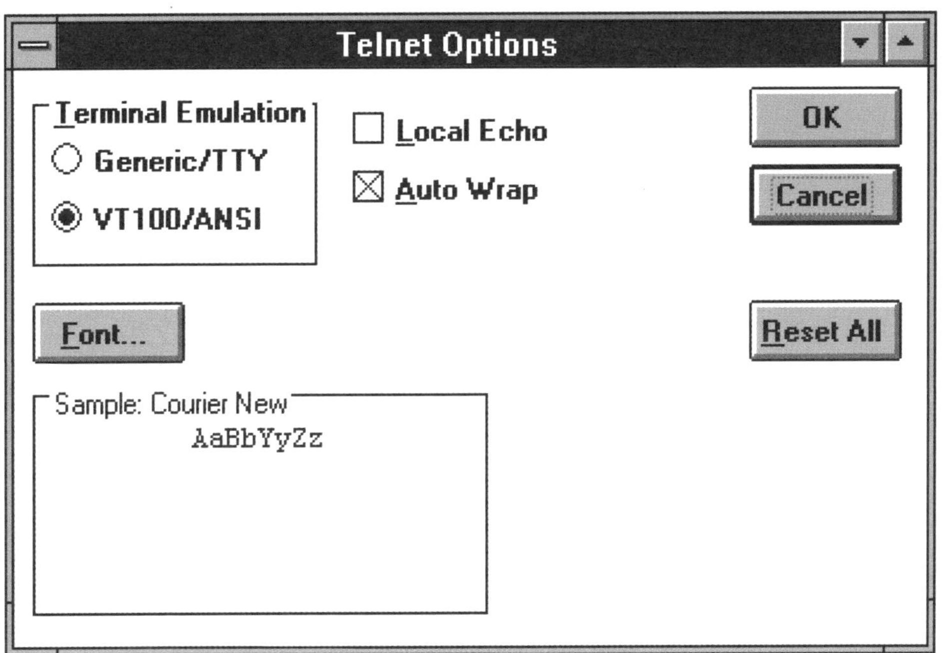

Local Echo controls the characters sent to the local computer. When using Telnet, select **Local Echo** *if no characters appear. The option is not selected by default.*

Telnet is a protocol

The protocol interprets commands from the local computer to execute on the remote

Terminal Emmulators simulate the remote's terminal

28 Telnet

❖ Connecting to a Host Computer

This lesson takes you through the steps for connecting to a Host computer via Telnet. A sports information host in Colorado will be used as the example.

Connecting to a Telnet Host

1. Click the **"Telnet - Log"** icon on the Toolbar; or click **Internet**, **Telnet** - **Remote Login**.
2. Type **"culine.colorado.edu"**, then press **TAB**. The "Port:" box is highlighted.
3. Type the port for the connection. Use **859** for the NBA; **860** for the NHL; **861** for MLB or **862** for the NFL.

Telnet Ports

> *Ports are used to route a connection to a certain area of the host, or to a different computer at the host domain.*

4. Press **ENTER** or click **OK**. The opening screen appears with a list of choices.

> *Remember that if a "Trying..." message appears but nothing else, network traffic may be too high. Close the window then try again later, or try another port number (when another port is an available option, as with this example).*

5. Type the letters for the team or league, etc. to see. For example: **sea** for Seattle.
6. Press **ENTER**.

> *To see different areas of the screen, click the* **arrows** *on the two vertical scroll bars to the right. The outer scroll bar is for the entire screen and the inner scroll bar is for the host's display. To change Telnet options within a Telnet session click* **Settings**, *then* **Telnet Options**. *Change the Options, then click* **OK**.

7. Type the letters of any other data you want to see, then press **ENTER**.

Quitting a Telnet Session

8. When done, type **"quit"** or **"q"**, then press **ENTER** to disconnect and close Telnet.

> *To book mark a host for later use, connect to the host using the World Wide Web browser, then "mark" the connection. Preface the host name with telnet:// within the browser. Note that a Login: name and Password: may be required. This method is useful for hosts that you have an account with or where a name and a password are known beforehand.*

Telnet

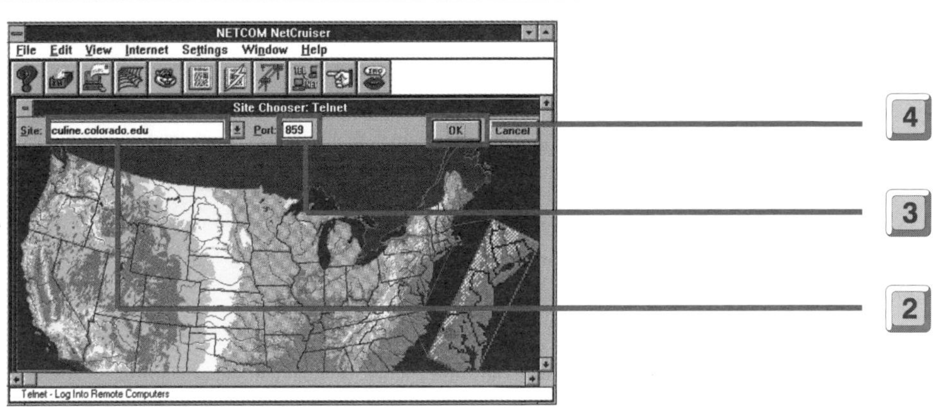

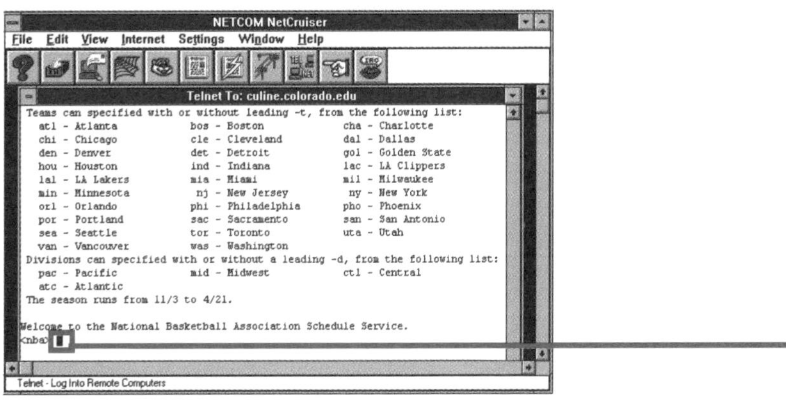

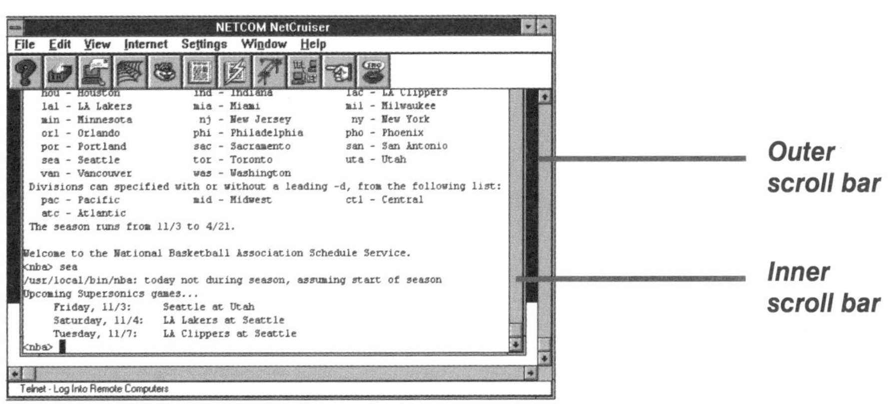

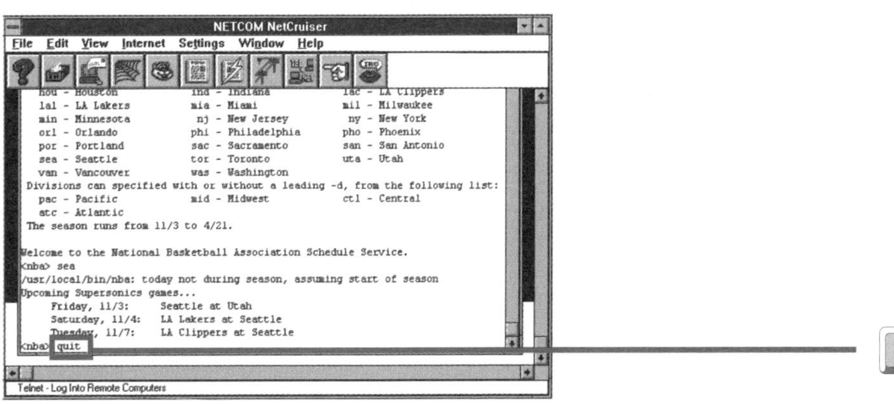

Quick Reference Bar

Click the "Telnet-Log Into..." icon to start Telnet

Click **Settings, Telnet Options** *to change settings*

Type **Quit** *then press* **Enter** *to end a session*

Finger

❖ The Finger Program

In order to send someone a message through the Internet you need their Email address. Of course not having this address presents a problem. When this occurs you may be able to use the Finger program and retrieve this information.

Finger Connections

1. The Finger program can connect to a remote computer and look up user information, such as their Email address. It will also let you know if a valid user is logged into the computer. To locate user information, enter the host name then the user name and the information you requested will appear.

Limitations

2. Unfortunately, not all users want their information public and some systems are not set up to allow this type of access. Estimates are that only one or two percent of Internet users can be found with Finger or other user information service. (Consequently, calling the person by phone and asking for their Email address is not a bad idea.)

3. Note that the Finger program cannot access IX.NETCOM.COM, nor can someone find your address through the Finger program. IX.NETCOM.COM is a server domain not a host computer. Your local computer is used as the host when logging into your NETCOM account, and it's IP address cannot be determined beforehand.

Other Resources

4. In the near future, a global X.500 directory will exist containing a list of Internet users and their addresses who want to be found. (Similar to the directory service for telephone numbers, information can remain private if so desired.) This directory is being created by the Internet Network Information Center in conjunction with AT&T.

5. Telnet to: **ds.internic.net** to get an idea of how the X.500 will appear. Login as "guest". Note that this system is not yet complete but you can still get an idea of its use.

6. Information about the InterNIC is available by sending Email to **info@internic.net**.

7. To include your name and Email address in the public directory, send a message to **admin@ds.internic.net** and ask to be put in the White Pages.

Finger

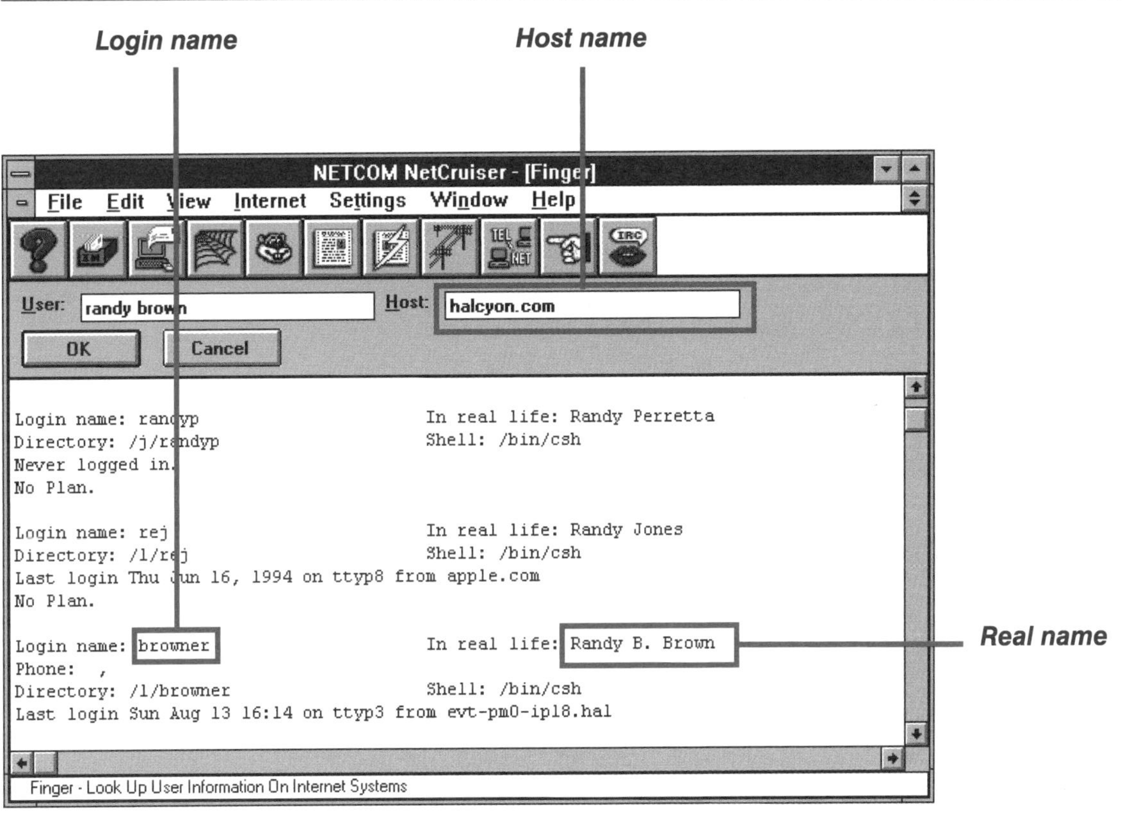

Randy Brown's Email address can be determined through his login and host names, separated by an "@" sign: browner@halcyon.com. But his host computer's name must be know, an example of Finger's limitation.

Quick Reference Bar

Finger looks up user information

Many systems do not allow Finger access

The X.500 directory may contain the information in question

Finger

❖ Using Finger to Find User Information

Run the Finger program and learn how to check for user information, as explained in this lesson.

Connecting to a Finger Host

1. Click the **"Finger - Look Up User Information On Internet Systems"** icon on the Toolbar; or click **Internet**, **Finger User Lookup**.

2. Type the host name in the "Site:" box, then press **ENTER**.

3. In the "User:" box, type the user name to look up.

> *The "User:" box usually contains the user's "real" name as they have registered for the service. To search the host computer for all names, leave the "User:" box empty.*

4. Press **ENTER** or click **OK**. If the message "Host... not found: Not an Internet Host" appears, you may have mistyped the host's name. Click **OK,** then enter the name again.

> *If a match is found, the user's information appears. You can increase the window size by clicking on the* ***up arrow*** *at the top right corner of the finger window. When an entire host is searched (no User: given), more than one screen full of information may appear. Click* ***Next*** *to see the next screen.*

Searching Another Host

5. To search another host or for another "User:" fill in the new "User:" and (or) "Site:" box, then click **OK**.

6. To close the Finger window, click **Cancel**.

Finger

INST

30

Quick Reference Bar

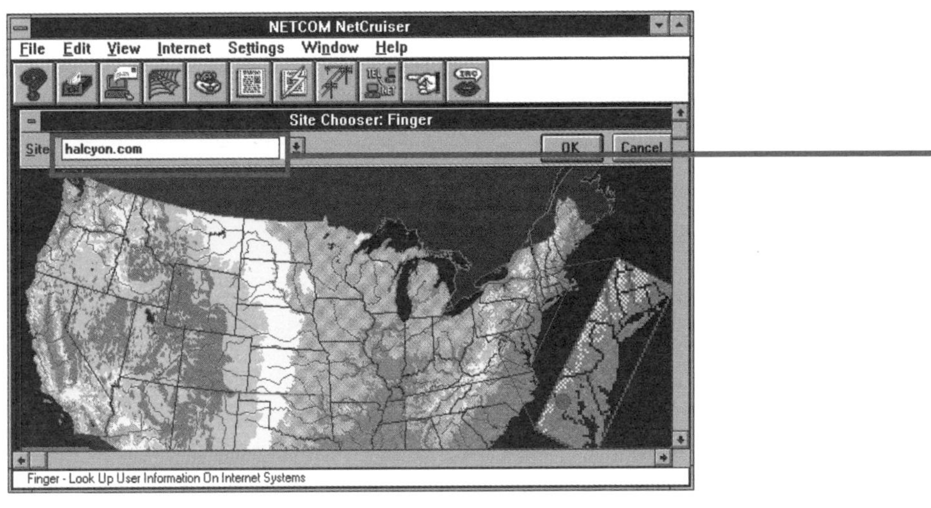

2

Click the "Finger-Look Up..." icon to start Finger

Type the host and user name to find

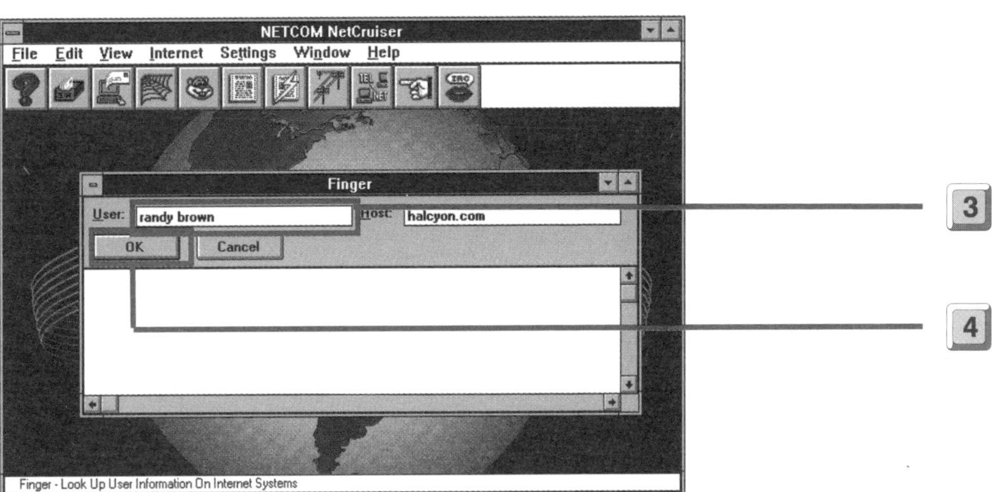

3

4

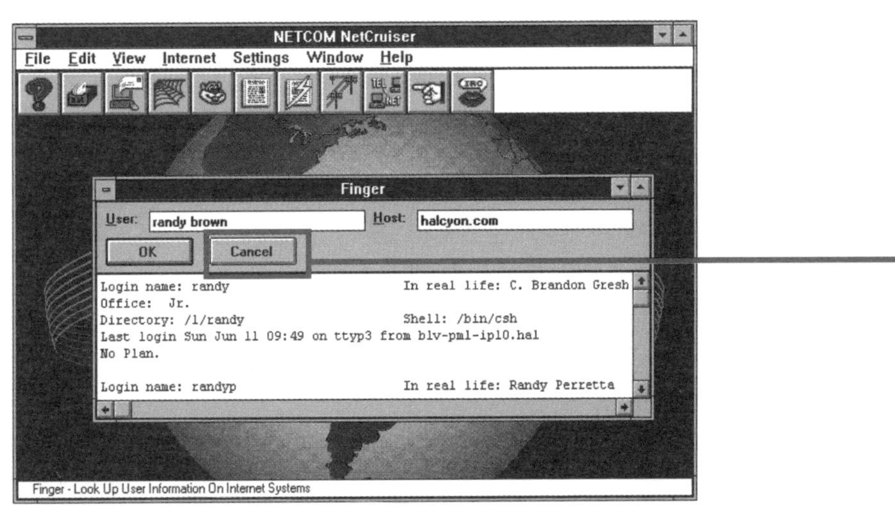

6

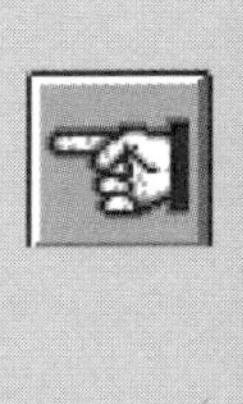

INST

31

Internet Relay Chat

❖ Understanding IRC

Internet Relay Chat, or IRC, is an on-line conversation between one or more persons on the Internet. Words are communicated by typing them in from the keyboard and are then sent to the person or persons at the remote location. Following are some of the details, limitations and uses of IRC.

IRC Connections

1. Users wanting to participate in an IRC "chat" connect to a host computer providing the service. Information is then exchanged between the active participants.

2. IRC is similar to a telephone party line. Each person has their own line (connection) to interact with others sending their thoughts across the line. IRC is also similar to UseNet groups, except topics are discussed "live" or in "real time" mode.

Uses

3. Used as a recreational communications system, IRC is great for meeting people and having fun. Still, nothing prevents businesses form using the service for meetings, seminars or other activities. However, most businesses prefer a more private method for communications.

4. Many college students use IRC as a substitute for long-distance telephone calls. Internet connections are free at some educational institutions.

Addresses and Ports

5. IRC connections can be within or outside of the NETCOM community. If you come across an IRC host that is of interest but outside of NETCOM, you can connect to this host via NetCruiser. You will need the host's address and port number for this use. Note that the default port number of 6667 is used for most hosts. If different, the port number will be provided along with the host's name.

Channels

6. IRC connections take place in channels. Think of channels as different topics or groups. With NetCruiser you can join up to five IRC channels during a session.

Rules

7. Rules governing IRC chats and the way that commands are entered can be difficult for most new users. Study these rules before going "live" in a conversation. Files are available to assist in this matter as described in the next lesson. NetCruiser's on-line Help file also contains useful information for IRC.

Internet Relay Chat

Quick Reference Bar

IRC requires a host computer providing this service

Participants communicate by typing words from their keyboard

IRC connections take place in channels

Channels represent topics or groups

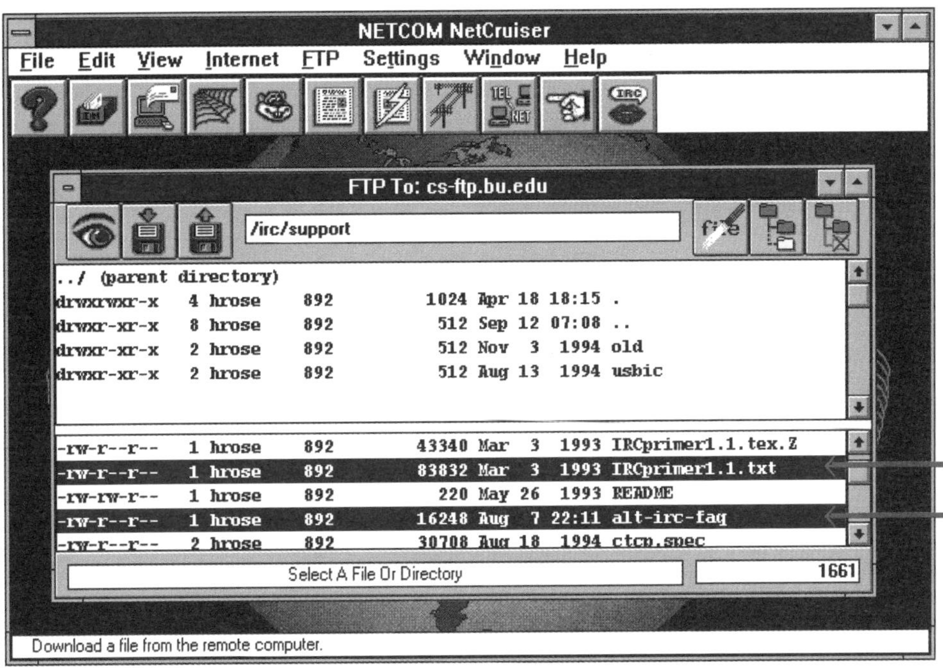

Files available via FTP

Information available through NetCruiser's on-line help

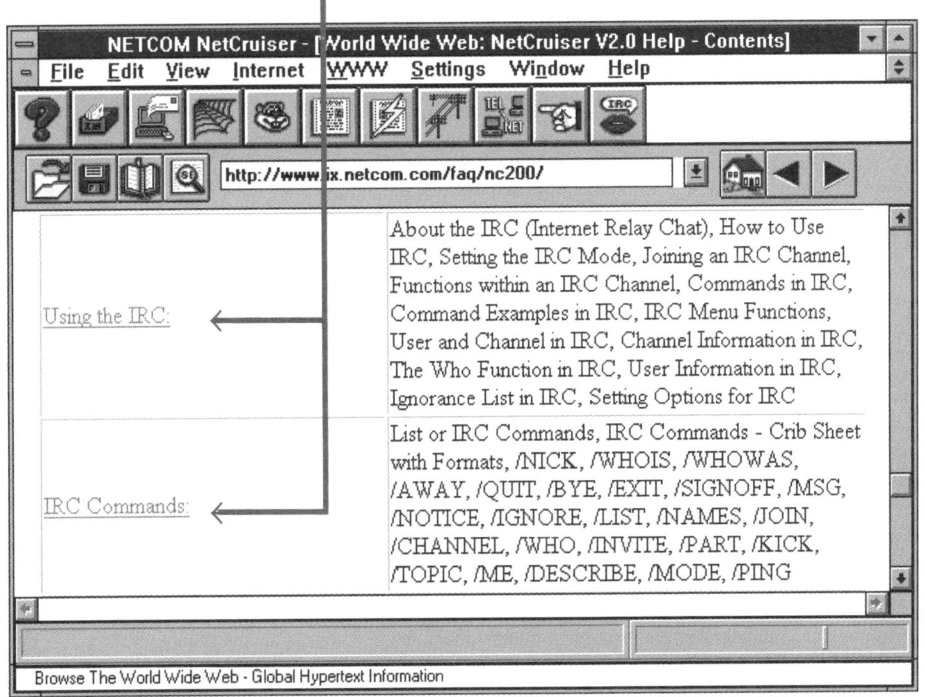

Internet Relay Chat

❖ Connecting to an IRC Host

An understanding of the rules and regulations of IRC should be known before participating in a "live" session. In other words, users should know what they are getting into before jumping in. This lesson takes you through the basic steps of connecting to an IRC host but does not go through an actual interaction with others. You can do this later after learning the basics of IRC. You will also be directed in where to download a file via FTP, an excellent learning tool of this service.

Starting the IRC Client

1 Click the **"IRC Chat With Internet Users All Over The World"** icon on the Toolbar; or click **Internet, IRC - Internet Relay Chat**.

The IRC options appear. You can connect only to "NETCOM IRC Hosts" (the default), or an "Other IRC Host." Leave as is for this lesson. Later, if you click the "Other IRC Host" option, a prompt appears for the host's address and port. Leave the port as 6667 unless otherwise noted. When using the "NETCOM IRC Hosts" option, click the **drop-down arrow** in the "Please make a selection" box, then click **NETCOM Private** for exclusive NETCOM connections.

Nicknames

2 Set your nickname. Click to the right of the name in the "Nickname:" box. Press the **BACKSPACE** key to remove the name. Now type your nickname.

Most people use nicknames when IRCing (pronounced IRKing). Nicknames for IRC are similar to the ones used in the days of CB radio popularity. Type in your real name if you cannot think of one at the moment. One can always be entered later. Up to nine characters can be used.

3 Type your name in the "**Your Name:**" box.

4 Click **Save Setting** to save the changes.

5 Click **Connect**. A connection is made to the IRC host and its opening screen is shown. Increase the window size if desired. Click the **up arrow** at the top right of the IRC window.

Connecting

IRC Text Box

A text box appears at the bottom of the screen. The box is used for typing in the text to send to remote users. To increase its size, move the mouse to the top line of the box and hold it there until the cursor turns into an up and down arrow. Now click and hold down the mouse button until the line turns into a thick line (release and try again if this doesn't occur). Keep the mouse button held down then drag the line upward to the desired size. Release the mouse.

IRC Information File

The upper portion of the window displays the number of users and operators on-line. Also included is a reference to FTP servers where files can be downloaded. FTP to the server: cs-ftp.bu.edu, then open the directories /irc then /support. Note the difference in this address and the one on the screen. Do not include the :/irc/support/ part in the FTP server address. Download the files: IRCprimer1.1.txt, and ALT-IRC-FAQ

Quitting an IRC Session

6 Quit the IRC connection. Type **"/quit"**, then press **ENTER**. Click **Yes**.

Internet Relay Chat

Quick Reference Bar

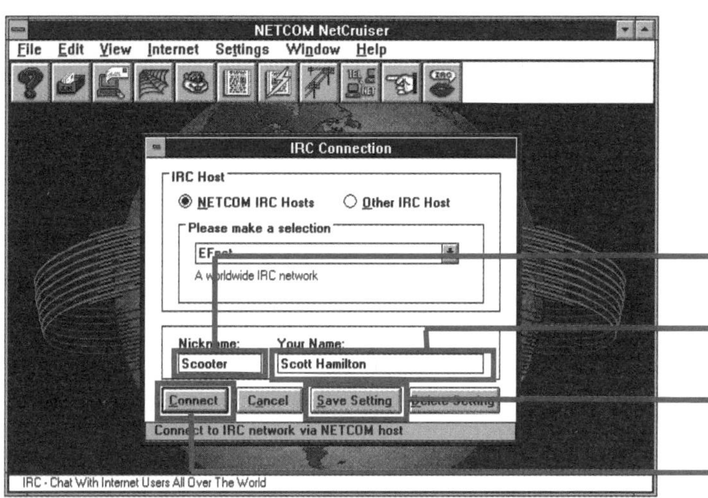

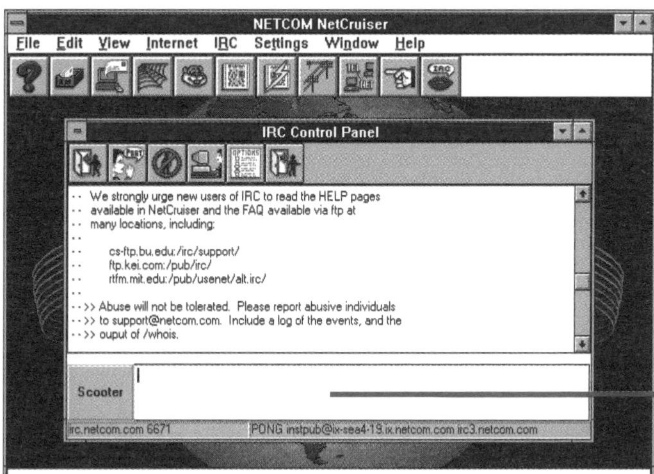

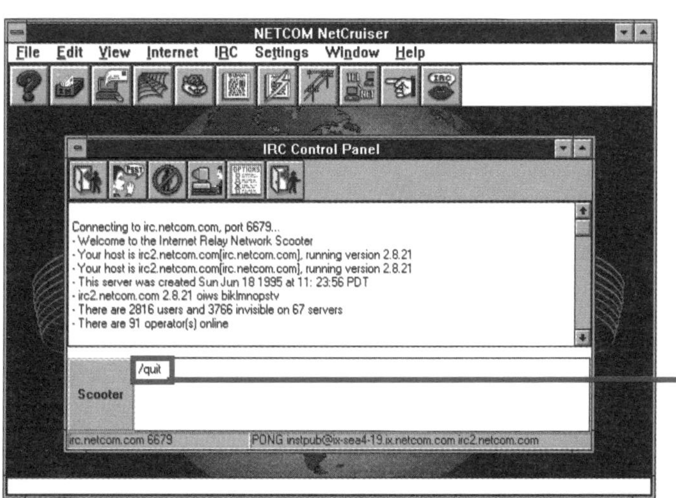

Click the "IRC Chat..." icon to start IRC

Click **Connect** *to reach an IRC host*

Type **"/Quit"** *then press* **ENTER** *to disconnect*

Housekeeping

❖ Setting Startup Options

You will probably use one of the NetCruiser applications more often than the others. Email for example is used almost exclusively by many users. For efficiency this or any other application may be run upon startup as described in the steps below.

Viewing Startup Options

1. Close any open applications like Email, UseNet, etc. Click their **Control** button, then **Close**; or press **CTRL+F4**. Do this for each open application.

2. Click **Settings**, then **Startup Options**.

Selecting a Startup Application

3. Click the radio button to the left of the "Application" used most often. (Feel free to leave as the default of "None" if this is preferred.)

4. Click **OK**. The selected application will run at startup the next time NetCruiser runs and makes an Internet connection.

The "Autoload Netcom's winsock.dll" option is required to run non-NetCruiser applications with NetCruiser. For example, other Email programs like Eudora, or other World Wide Web browsers like Netscape. Click this option if other applications are used. Start NetCruiser again to make effective.

Housekeeping

Quick Reference Bar

Click **Settings, Startup Options** *to select a startup application*

Rerun NetCruiser to make effective

Press **CTRL+F4** *to close applications*

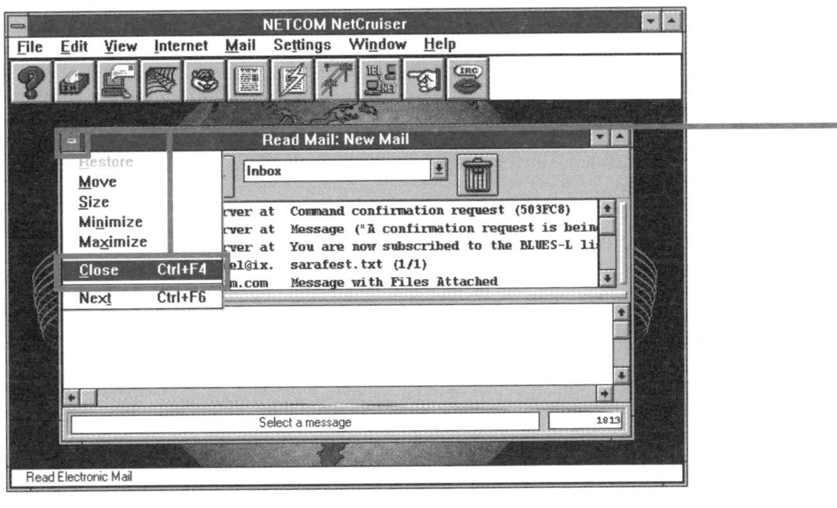

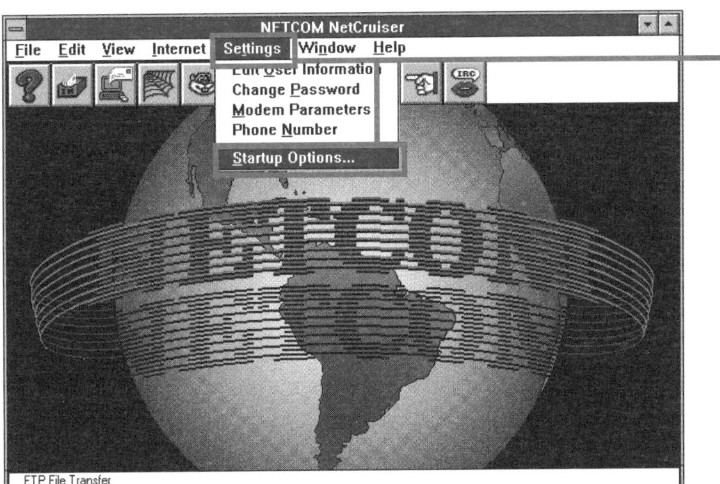

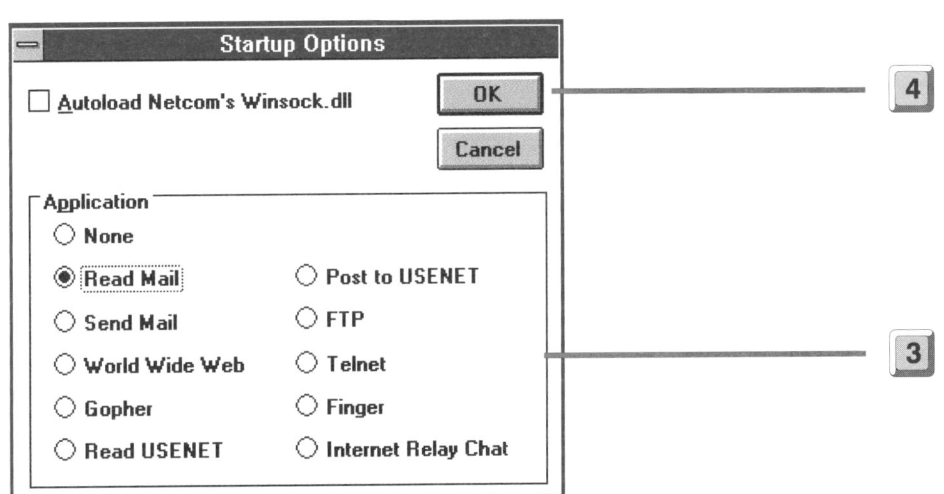

Housekeeping

❖ Checking Internet Usage Times

Knowing how much "prime time" remains on your monthly account can help in planning your Internet connection times. This simple lesson takes you through the steps of reviewing a break down of your Internet usage.

1. Click **Help**, then **Session Summary**. A summary of your usage time appears.

Viewing the Monthly Summary

2. Review the summary.

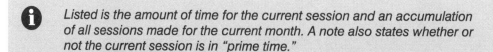

Listed is the amount of time for the current session and an accumulation of all sessions made for the current month. A note also states whether or not the current session is in "prime time."

3. Close the summary window. Click its **Control** button, then **Close**.

Housekeeping

Quick Reference Bar

Click **Help, Session Summary** *to view usage times*

Press **CTRL+F4** *to close the Session Summary*

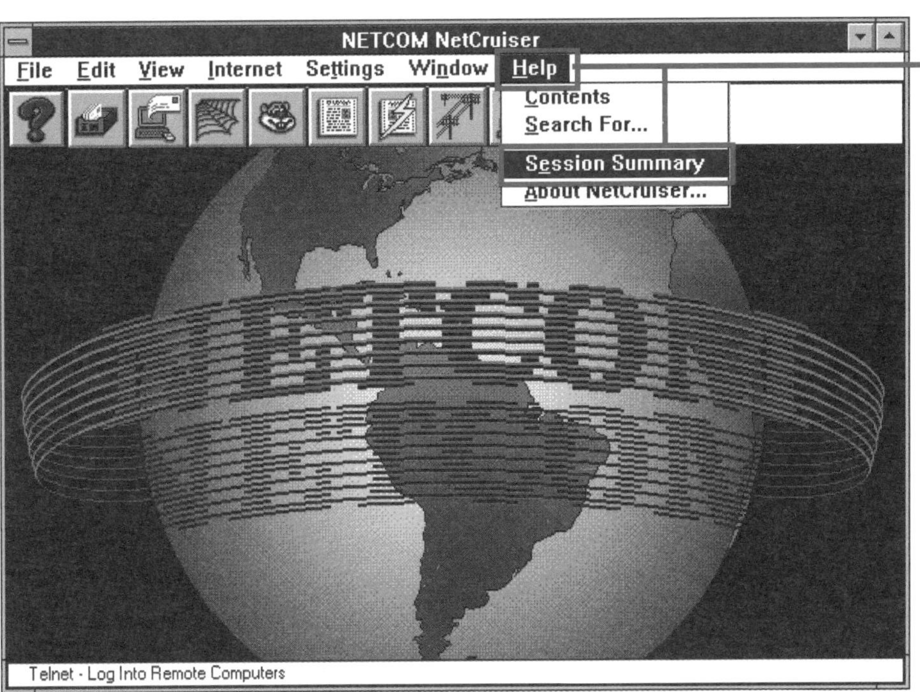

1

3

Session Summary: instpub (Anthony Difrancia)

Your Internet Email Address

instpub@ix.netcom.com

Connect Time And Prime Time

Free Prime Time Left This Month:	**22:25:52**	
Currently Prime Time:	**No**	
	Current Session	This Month
Prime Time Used:	**00:00:00**	**17:34:08**
Total Time Connected:	**00:05:40**	**29:38:41** in **60** sessions

times are approximate and given in the format hours:minutes:seconds

Session Summary Retrieved At

8:30:38 AM, Monday, September 11, 1995 NETCOM, Seattle WA
8:31:12 PM, Tuesday, September 12, 1995 Local PC

Housekeeping

❖ Upgrading NetCruiser

When NETCOM develops new upgrades to the NetCruiser program they make it available through an Internet connection. This lesson takes you through the steps of updating NetCruiser when needed. Note that at the time of this writing the version provided with this training guide is current. No update is needed. Refer to this lesson when you get word of an available upgrade.

Starting the Upgrade

1. Close any open applications like Email, UseNet, etc. Click their **control** button, then **Close**.

2. Click **File**, **Download new version**. A window appears showing the "Download length:" in bytes and the "Estimated time:" for the download.

> *A message will appear if you already have the latest version. Cancel the download if this occurs. Click* **OK**, *then* **Exit**.

Downloading the Upgrade

3. Click **Download** to begin the process. A "% complete" status shows and the byte count increases. Wait until the download completes.

4. Click **OK**.

5. Click **Upgrade**. A message states that all running sessions will be closed and asks if you want to continue.

6. Click **Yes**. A "NetCruiser Upgrade" window appears. Click **Exit** to bypass the upgrade (an upgrade can be done later), or click **Upgrade** to continue.

Release Notes

7. If Upgrade is selected in step 6, an "NCSETUP Upgrade Complete" status box appears. Click **OK**. A "Release Notes..." window appears.

8. Read the notes. Click the **arrow** on the vertical scroll bar if it is not all visible. (The release notes are stored as a file in the \Netcom directory. Look for the file: release.txt.)

9. Click **Exit** and (or) close the release notes window. Click its **Control** button, then **Close**. If desired, run NetCruiser again and reconnect.

Housekeeping

Quick Reference Bar

Close all applications

Click File, Download New Version

A message appears if latest version is in use

Release notes are stored in "\Netcom"

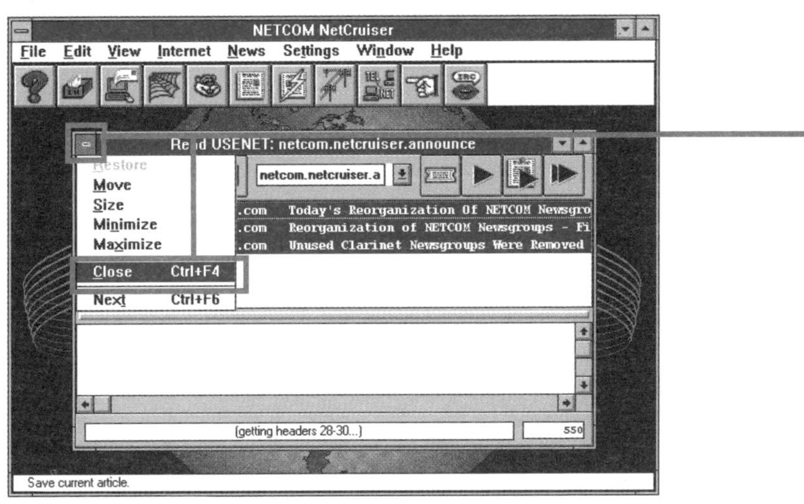

1

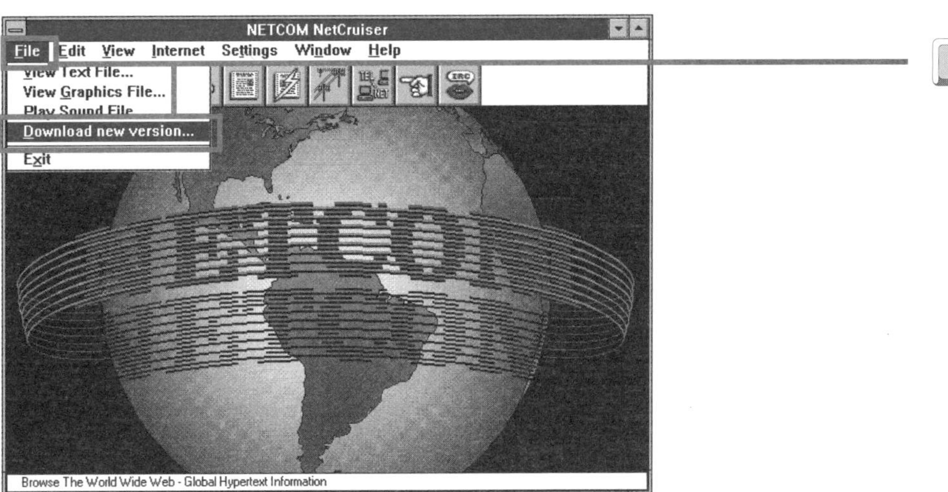

2

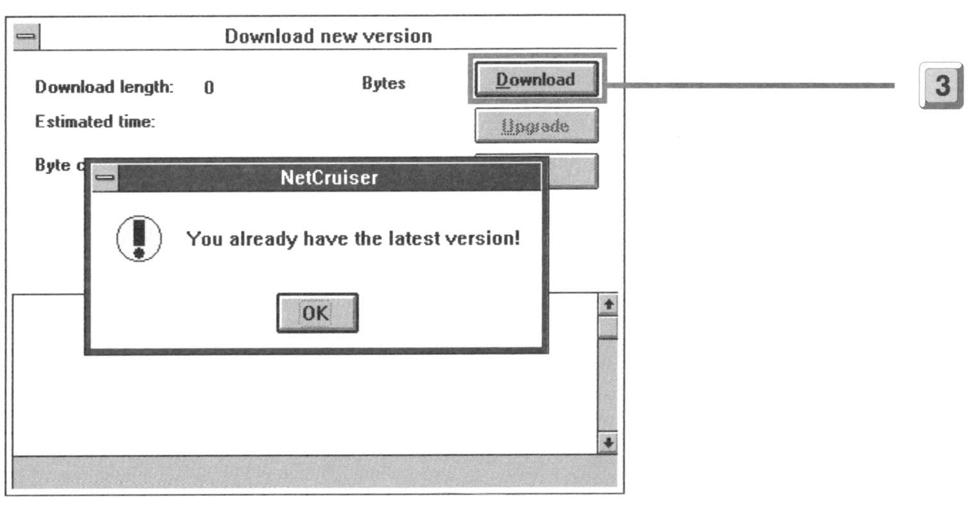

3

INST

36

Housekeeping

❖ Backing up Files

Along with keeping your NetCruiser software up to date, backing up its important files is recommended. Use the Windows File Manager or other program to perform the backup. The DOS COPY command can also be used. See the Windows or DOS User's Guide for further instructions. Following are the recommended files to back up. If anything happens to the original NetCruiser files (the ones within \Netcom), you can reinstall NetCruiser then copy the backup files to their appropriate location.

Important NetCruiser Files

1. **NETCOM.INI** — Located in the \Windows directory. Stores information relating to NetCruiser's configuration.
2. **MYGROUPS.NWS** — Located in the \Netcom directory. Stores the "Subscribed" Newsgroups.
3. **NETCOM.BM** — Located in the \Netcom directory. Stores the "book mark" sites.
4. **MAIL.SIG** — Located in the \Netcom directory. The signature file for outgoing Email.
5. **NEWS.SIG** — Located in the \Netcom directory. The signature file for outgoing Newsgroup articles.
6. **ADDRBOOK.DAT** — Located in the \Netcom directory. Stores Address Book entries.

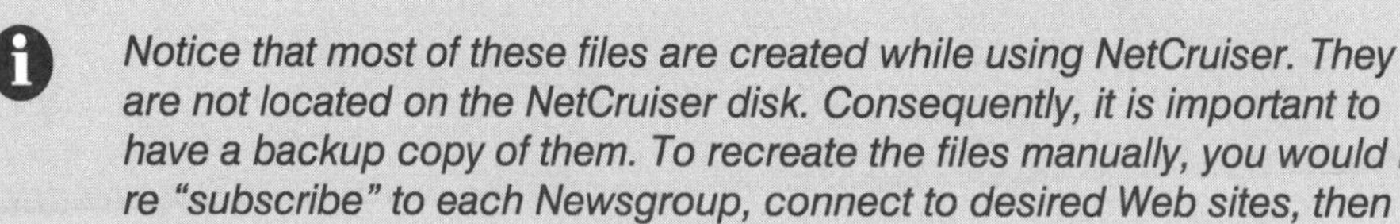

Notice that most of these files are created while using NetCruiser. They are not located on the NetCruiser disk. Consequently, it is important to have a backup copy of them. To recreate the files manually, you would have to re "subscribe" to each Newsgroup, connect to desired Web sites, then "book mark" recreate the signature files and retype Address Book entries.

Housekeeping

Open directory

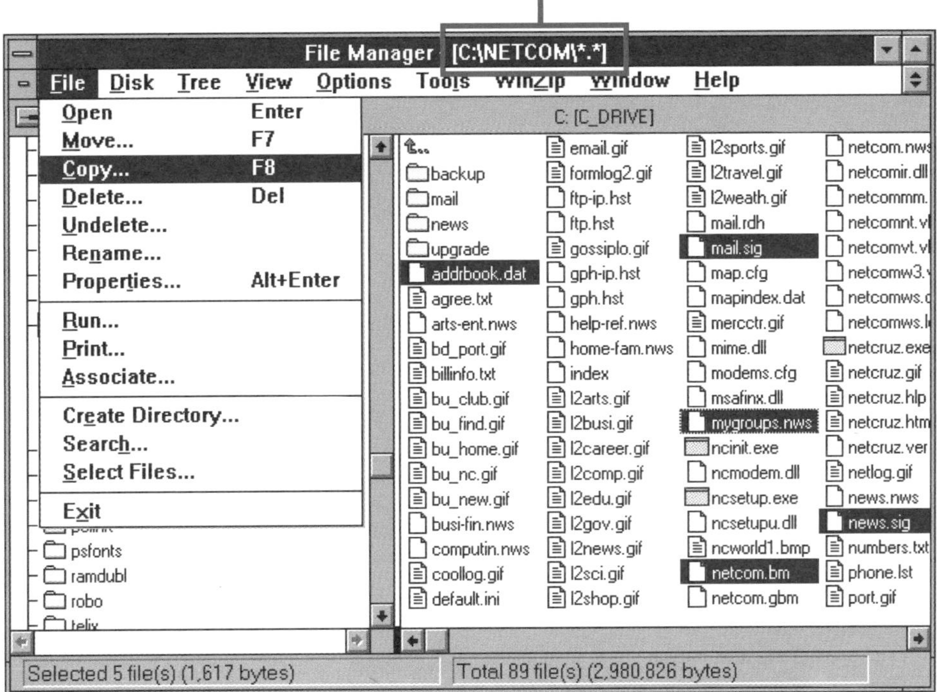

Open directory

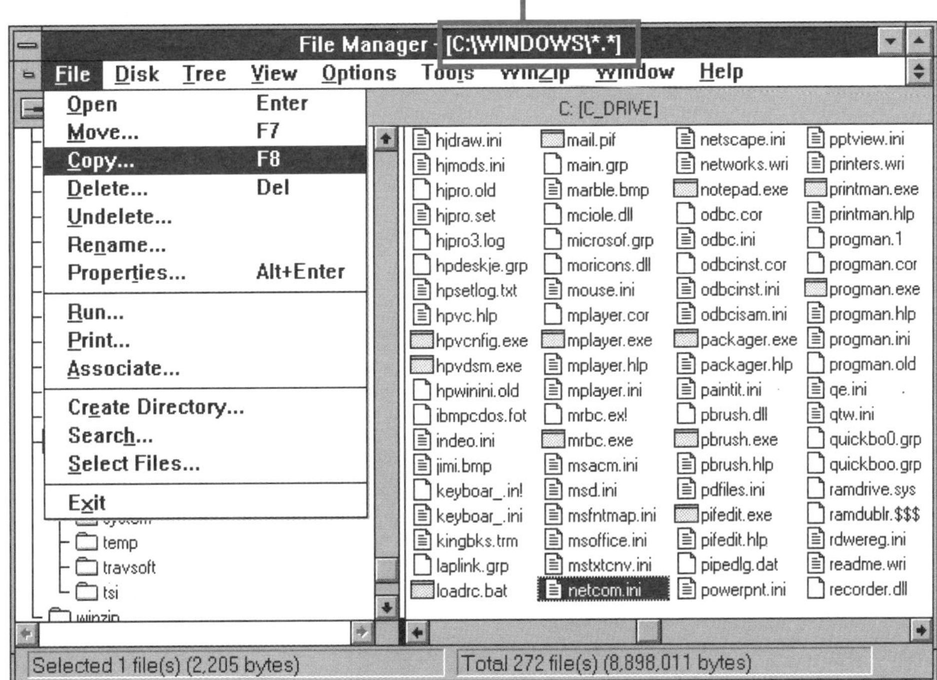

Important files in /Netcom directory: **mygroups .nws, Netcom .bm, addrbook .dat, mail.sig, news.sig**

Important files in \Windows directory: **netcom .ini**

Start File Manager from the Main Windows group

Press and hold down the CTRL key to select multiple files

Appendix A

Glossary

INST Dictionary of Terms

1.44 MB micro Diskette - Is a magnetic diskette for storing and retrieving electronic data and programs. It was introduced in the late 1980's as a high density 3.5" diskette. It has a data storage capacity of 1.44 megabytes. A 1.44MB micro diskette that has been formatted with a 1.44MB high density drive cannot be read or reliably written to with a 720K diskette drive. Because the two disk drives and diskettes appear to be identical, this is often a confusing matter for beginners. The 1.44MB micro diskette drives, however, can also read and write 720K diskettes.

Acknowledgment - A response sent by a receiver to indicate successful reception of information.

Active - A window or dialog box that is currently in use. Called the current window when a document is displayed.

Address - A numeric value assigned to a computer much like a telephone number is assigned to a home.

Advanced Networks and Services - (ANS) A company that owns and operates ANSNET, a major Wide Area Network in the Internet.

Alphanumeric - The term alphanumeric refers to data or terms that consist of both numbers and alphabetic characters (Examples of alphanumeric terms: WD40, 51VE, 2x4, R2D2, RU469, ICU812, OCT90, 1040EZ).

Analog - Any representation of information in which the amount of a substance or signal is proportional to the information represented.

Analog-to-Digital Converter - 9A-to-D converter) An electronic component that converts an analog electrical signal into a sequence of numbers.

ANSNET - A major Wide area Network that forms part of the Internet. ANSNET is owned by Advanced Networks and Services.

Application - Software designed to carry out a certain kind of action or activity, such as word processing, electronic mail, or spreadsheet entries. Sometimes called a program.

Archie - An automated search service available on the Internet that finds all files with a given name. The name archie is short for archive.

Archive Site - A site that records files for users to retrieve, either via FTP or email.

Attributes - The elements that determine the appearance of a character (bold, italic, 10pt) or a graphic (fill, line width, background color).

ANSI - ANSI is an abbreviation for American National Standards Institute. It is a non-governmental organization founded in 1918 that proposes, modifies, approves and publishes data processing standards for voluntary use in the United States. ANSI is also the U.S. representative to the International Standards Organization (ISO) in Paris and the International Electrotechnical Commission (IEC). Any programming language that claims to conform to ANSI standards must pass all the tests for the standard syntax rules as set forth by ANSI.

ARPA - Advanced Research Projects Agency. The governmental organization responsible for creating the beginnings of the Internet.

ARPAnet - The proto-Internet network created by ARPA.

ASCII - The American Standard Code for Information Interchange is a standard seven-bit code that was created in 1965 by Robert W. Bemer to achieve compatibility between various data processing equipment. ASCII (pronounced "ask-key") is the common code for microcomputer equipment. The Standard ASCII Character Set consists of 128 decimal numbers from zero through 127 assigned to letters, numbers, punctuation marks and the most common special characters. The Extended ASCII Character Set also consists of 128 decimal numbers and range from 128 through 255 representing additional special, mathematical, graphic and foreign characters.

AtoB (pronounced "a to b") - A UNIX program that turns ASCII files into binary files.

AUTOEXEC. BAT - The AUTOEXEC.BAT file is an operating system file that DOS searches for each time the microcomputer is booted. DOS only looks for it in the root directory of the boot device (either the A: floppy drive or the C: hard drive). The AUTOEXEC.BAT file is an ASCII text file and can be changed with any text editor program such as EDIT. Since the DOS commands in the AUTOEXEC.BAT are executed each time the system is booted, the operating environment for each particular system can be optimized to take advantage of the attached hardware. Software applications that reside on the hard disk often require that certain parameters be defined in the DOS environment space. These SET commands can be placed in the AUTOEXEC.BAT file.

Appendix A

Back Up - To save copies of files for safekeeping. You can back up files as you work on them to protect your work in case of a power failure or a machine problem.

Bandwidth - Information theory used to express the amount of information that can flow through a given point at any given time. It is the capacity of a network, usually measured in bits per second. Some points have narrow bandwidth (indicating not much information can flow through at one time), and others have high bandwidth (indicating a great deal of information can flow through at one time). Network systems need higher bandwidth for audio or video than for e-mail or other services.

Batch File - A DOS file that contains several commands that are carried out when the batch file name is entered at the DOS prompt. All batch files have a .BAT extension. Batch files are useful when you need to type the same series of DOS commands repeatedly.

Baud (Pronounced "bawd") - The conventional unit of measurement used to described data transmission speed. One baud is one bit per second.

BIOS - The Basic Input/Output System or the part of the computer operating system that communicates with the screen, the keyboard, printers and other peripheral devices.

Binary digit (bit) - Either a 0 or 1. The Internet uses binary digits to represent information, including: audio, text, and video. Any file that contains nontextual data. In FTP, a command that tells FTP to transfer information as an arbitrary stream of bits rather than as a series of textual characters.

Binary File - Although all files are encoded in binary, the term is used to refer to nontext files. the distinction is especially pertinent to FTP.

Bits Per Second (bps) - Literally, a measure of the rate of data transmission. Usually, the measure refers to the capacity of a network or the measurement of modem transmission speed.

Body - The part of an email message where you type your message, as opposed to the header or the signature.

Bookmark - A facility in the gopher service that can record the location of a particular menu, making it possible to return to the menu later.

Bounce - What email does when it doesn't go through.

Browsing - The act of looking through information by repeatedly scanning and selecting.

BtoA (pronounced "b to a") - A UNIX program that turns binary files into ASCII files for transmission via email.

BTW - Abbreviation for "By the Way"

Buffer - A temporary data storage area in your computer's memory. A buffer is needed to compensate for differences in speed between computer components.

Bullet - A symbol, such as a filled circle, that may precede each item in a list.

Button - A graphical representation of an option or a command that activates the option or executes the command when selected.

Bulletin Board Service (BBS) - A service that permits one person to post a message for others to read. Each bulletin board contains discussion of a single topic. A bulletin board is sometimes called a computer conference.

Byte - The amount of space needed to store a single character (number, letter code). A byte generally represents eight binary digits (bits). 1024 bytes equals one kilobytes (K).

Cache - A buffer area in a computer or a special section of random access memory (RAM) that is continually updated to contain recently accessed contents of main storage to reduce access time while a program is running.

Card - A removable printed circuit board that is plugged into an expansion slot (such as a graphics card, clock card, sound card or fax card).

Carrier - A steady electrical signal or tone that is used by a modem to encode information for transmission across a communication line or a telephone connection. A carrier is the tone heard when a computer uses a modem to communicate over a telephone connection.

CD-ROM (Compact Disk-Read Only Memory) - A read only optical storage technology that uses compact disks as a means of data storage. A single CD-ROM disk can hold over 650 megabytes of information or half a billion characters of text. Unlike floppy disks, most CD-ROM disks can be read from but not written to.

CFV - What you do after discussing whether a new newsgroup should be created. Abbreviation for "Call For Votes."

Charter - The document that lays out what topics a newsgroup will cover, what its name will be, and other relevant details.

Appendix A

Chat Script - A simple conversation between your computer and your host machine that allows you to log in automatically.

Chip - A chip is an integrated circuit created on a tiny silicon flake. The chip can be used as the main memory or as the Central Processing Unit (CPU). When both memory and logic capabilities are contained on the same chip it is called a microprocessor or a computer on a chip. The chip consumes very little power. It is compact, inexpensive and can process a million or more instructions per second.

Click - To press and release a mouse button (usually the left button) once.

Client - A program that uses the Internet to contact a remote server. Usually, a separate client program is needed for each Internet service.

Client-Server Computing - The interaction between two programs when they communicate across a network.

Clipboard - An area of memory, also called a buffer, where text, graphics and commands can be stored to await further action. It is a temporary holding place for items that have been cut or copied. The item remains on the Clipboard until you cut or copy an additional item or until you turn off the computer. If you are using a Shell, the Clipboard can be used to cut and paste information from one program into another.

COM Port - A communications channel or pathway over which data is transferred between remote computing devices. IBM-compatible microcomputer operating under DOS can have as many as four COM Ports; COM1, COM2, COM3 and COM4. These COM ports are actually serial ports most often used with a modem to establish a communication channel via a telephone line. The COM ports are also used to send data to a serial printer or to connect a serial mouse.

Command Line - Where you type commands to an operating system like DOS or UNIX. Command-line operating systems can be powerful but are often a difficult to work with.

Compress - To make a file smaller by removing redundant information. Specifically, the UNIX program that does just that. Files compress with the UNIX compress command end with a .Z suffix.

Computer Network - A hardware mechanism that computers use to communicate. A network is classified as a Local Area Network or Wide Area Network, depending on the hardware capabilities.

Connect Time - The amount of time you are actually connected to and using a computer. This is the time that your connect or telephone charges are based on.

CONFIG.SYS - The CONFIG.SYS file is an operating system file that DOS searches for each time the microcomputer is booted. It is not required but provides many advantages. DOS only looks for it in the root directory of the boot device (either the A: floppy drive or the C: hard drive). Since the DOS commands in the CONFIG.SYS are executed each time the system is booted, the operating environment for each particular system can be optimized to take advantage of the attached hardware. The CONFIG.SYS file is an ASCII text file and can be changed with any text editor program such as EDIT. In order for the changes to take affect, the system must be re-booted.

Connection - When two programs communicate using TCP, the TCP software on the two machines forms a connection across the Internet similar to a telephone call.

Conversion - A process by which files created in one application are changed to a format that can be used in another application.

Current Directory - The directory at the end of the current directory path. It is the directory that is searched first for a requested file and where a file is stored if you don't specify a path.

Cursor - A symbol (usually a blinking horizontal or vertical bar) that designates the position on the screen where text or codes will be inserted or deleted.

DARPA - Defense Advance Research Projects Agency. Replaced ARPA and has a more military bent.

Database - A database is a set of interrelated data records stored on a direct access storage device in a data structure that is designed to allow multiple applications to access the information. A database should have minimal redundancy of data and allow for growth and change. A database is a highly structured file that attempts to provide all the information allocated to a particular subject and to allow programs to access only those items they need.

Default - A program's predetermined setting or action that takes effect unless specifically changed.

Delimiter - Most commonly used to refer to a character or code that marks the beginning or end of an item such as a sentence, paragraph, page, record, field, or word. Also used in "dynamic delimiter" to refer to a character that expands to enclose part of an equation.

Appendix A

Demodulation - The process of extracting information from a modulated signal that arrives over transmission line or telephone connection. Demodulation usually occurs in a device called a modem.

Demodulator - The electronic device in a modem that decodes an incoming signal and extracts data.

Deselect - To remove the X from a check box, or to remove a check mark from a menu item.

Dialup - To call another computer via modem. The term is often lumped together as one word.

Destination Address - A numeric value in a packet that specifies the computer to which the packet has been sent. The destination address in a packet traveling across the Internet is the IP address of the destination computer.

Device Driver - A device driver is a system file or software component that contains the instructions necessary to control the operation of a peripheral device. It contains the detailed information about the device it controls. The standard device drivers are part of the operating system and additional drivers are added as new peripheral devices are installed. (Example: if a mouse or trackball is added to your personal computer, the appropriate device driver needs to be installed so that the operating system can communicate properly with it). Device drivers associated with application packages such as desktop publishing programs typically only perform the data translation. These higher level drivers rely on the standard drivers to actually send the data to the device (printer, plotter, CD-ROM).

Dialog Box - A means of communication with a program. A dialog box displays warnings and messages and lets you select and implement options by choosing appropriate command buttons.

Dial Up - To call another computer via modem. The term is often lumped together as one word.

Dialup - A connection or line reached by modem, as in "a dialup line."

Digital - Any technology that uses numbers to represent information. A computer is inherently digital because it represents keystrokes, pictures, text, and sound using numbers.

Digital-to-Analog Converter - (D-to-A converter) An electronic device that converts a sequence of numbers into an analog electrical signal. A D-to-A-Converter is needed to change the numbers on a compact disc into sounds.

Dimmed - The appearance of an icon, a command, or a button that cannot be chosen or selected.

Directory - A directory is an area on a disk for storing files. Directories consist of files and /or sub-directories. A directory listing will show the names of files and subdirectories subordinate to that directory along with file sizes, creation dates and times.

Domain Name - The name assigned to a computer on the Internet. A single computer's name can contain multiple strings separated by periods. Domain names often end in .com or .edu.
DOS (Disk Operating System) - Software that oversees disk I/O, video support, keyboard control and internal commands. A computer needs a disk operating system to function.

DOS Prompt - The on-screen characters, such as "C:\.", indicating that you can enter DOS commands or a program name.

Dot Pitch - The sharpness of the images that appear on your computer monitor is defined by the dot pitch. Dot pitch measures the width of the dots that make up a pixel. The smaller the dot pitch, the sharper the image. Color monitors use three dots in red, green and blue (RGB) to focus on a single point or dot to make up a pixel. On monochrome monitors, each dot is a pixel. The accepted standard dot pitch is 31/100 of a millimeter (.31mm) or .31 dot pitch (DP).

Double-Click - To press and release the mouse button twice in rapid succession.

Download - To retrieve a file from another machine, usually a host machine, to your machine.

Drag - To move text or an object. To move the mouse pointer while holding down the mouse button. Position the pointer on the item you want to move, press and hold down the left mouse button, move the mouse, then release the mouse button.

E-mail Address - Each user is assigned an electronic mailbox address. To send e-mail, a user must enter the e-mail address of the recipient. On the Internet, e-mail addresses usually have the form person@computer.

Emoticons - Another name for smileys.

Electronic mail (e-mail) - A service that permits one to send a memo to another person, a group, or a computer program. Electronic mail software also permits one to reply to a memo.

Ergonomics - The study of human posture and proportion in order to design furniture and equipment that can be used comfortably and without strain. It is frequently called human engineering and emphasizes the safety, comfort and ease-of-use of human operated machines, such as computer workstations.

Appendix A

Expanded Memory - Expanded memory refers to memory that acts as a pool which can be mapped into one or more conventional memory areas. Unlike extended memory, expanded memory is available for all processor types. It requires a special device driver and conforms to a standard developed by Lotus, Intel and Microsoft Corporations. This standard enables the programs that recognize the standard to work with more than 640K RAM under DOS.

Extended Memory - Extended Memory is available only with the (80)286, (80)386, (80)486 or the Pentium P6 CPUs and refers to memory above 1 megabyte. It is directly addressable in protected mode. Under DOS, RAM disks or virtual disks can be created in extended memory but not used for processing. Extended memory is best utilized by operating systems running in protected mode such as UNIX and OS/2, or by operating environments running with DOS such as Windows, DESQview and Windows 95.

FAQ - Frequently Asked Question. Lists of these questions and answers to them are often posted in newsgroups to reduce the number of novice questions. Read a FAQ list before asking a question, to make sure yours isn't a frequently asked one.

Feed - Shorthand for a connection to another machine that sends you mail and news. I might say, "I have a mail feed from Ed's machine."

File Compression - The term "compression" means to reduce in size. Computer file compression is achieved with an archiving program. Files are quickly reduced in size. This process creates archive files which uses less disk space, individual files can be stuffed into a single archive file, and Archived files travel faster via modem.

Filename - The name given to a text, graphics or worksheet file which a program uses to open and save a file. The format varies with different operating systems.

File Server - A program running on a computer that provides access to files on that computer. The term is often applied loosely to computers that run file server programs.

File Transfer Protocol (FTP) - The Internet service used to transfer a copy of a file from one computer to another. After contacting a remote computer, a user must enter a login name and password; some FTP servers allow access to public files through the special login anonymous.

Finger - An Internet service used to determine which users are currently logged into a particular computer or to find out more about an individual user.

Font - A group of letters, numbers and symbols with a common typeface. Fonts are described by name, appearance and size, as in Helvetica Bold 10pt.

Formatting - The process of preparing a disk so that the operating system can find the sectors on each of the disk tracks. Formatting also establishes the File Allocation Table (FAT). A disk can not be used until it is formatted. Hard disks must be initialized or "low-level formatted" before they can be formatted. The low-level format sets up the sectors on a hard disk and maps the bad areas for the operating system to avoid. This process of low-level formatting is also called initializing, physical formatting or absolute formatting.

Function Keys - On personal computer keyboards there is a set of numbered keys called the function keys. On most keyboards there are either ten or twelve keys labeled F1 through F10 or F12 which are used to send different special purpose commands to the program in control. Function keys can be programmed to work by themselves or in conjunction with the Control, Alt, and Shift keys.

FYI - Abbreviation for "For your information."

GIF - Graphics Interchange Format. A platform-independent file format developed by CompuServe, the GIF format is commonly used to distribute graphics on the Internet.

Gigabyte - One Gigabyte equals 1 kilobyte times 1 megabyte. That's 1,073,741,824 bytes, or 2x30 power. 'Giga' is a binary analog to the U.S. decimal unit 'billion' The (80)286 microprocessor can access 1GByte of virtual memory. Compact disks (CD's) have storage capacities of over a gigabyte, which is the equivalent of fifty 20-megabyte hard disks.

Gopher - The name of an Internet browsing service in which all information is organized into a hierarchy of menus. Gopher displays a menu on the screen and allows the user to select an item. The selection either leads to a file of information or to another menu.

Handle - An on-screen marker, usually a small black square, that lets you size and manipulate an object or item in a drawing. Handles appear around selected objects. To use a handle, drag it with the mouse.

Hexadecimal - A numbering system based on 16 digits used in computer programming as a convenient shorthand for working with binary numbers. These 16 values or states are numbered 0123456789ABCDEF. Each hexa- decimal number can be presented as a four-bit code (0000 through 1111 in binary numbering).

Appendix A

Homepage - A page of information accessible through the World Wide Web. The page can contain a mixture of graphics and text, and can include embedded references to other such pages. Usually each user and each organization has a separate homepage.

Host - A synonym for user's computer. Hub - An electronic device that connects to several computers and replaces a LAN, usually an Ethernet. Hubs are used with 10base-T.

Hypermedia - An information storage system in which each page of information can contain embedded references to images, sounds, and other pages of information. When a user selects an item, the hypermedia system follows the associated reference.

Hypertext - A system for storing pages of textual information that each contain embedded references to other pages of information.

Icon - A small graphic image that represents a function, an object or a pointer tool. Clicking on the icon will produce an action.

IMHO - Abbreviation for "In my humble opinion."

Information Superhighway - A term used by the popular press to refer to the emerging national information infrastructure in the United States. The Internet is the first part of the information infrastructure, which is sometimes called the information highway.

Infrastructure - A service or facility that is fundamental to a society. Examples include systems for delivering food and water, transportation facilities, and telephones.

Interactive - You use the Internet interactively when you are working on it personally, browsing Gopherspace or searching an Archie database.

internet - With a lowercase *i*, an internet is a group of connected networks.

Internet - The collection of networks and routers that use the TCP/IP protocol suite and function as a single, large network. The Internet reaches government, commercial, and educational organization around the world.

Internet Address - Each computer attached to the Internet is assigned a unique IP address. Software uses the address to identify the intended recipient when it sends a message. An Internet address is also called an IP address.

Internet Architecture Board - A group of invited volunteers that manages certain aspects of the Internet, such as standards and address allocation.

IP - Internet Protocol. The main protocol used on the Internet.

Justification - The alignment of multiple lines of text along the left margin, the right margin, or both margins.

KBPS (Kilo Bits Per Second) - A measure of the rate of data transmission equal to 1000 bps.

LISTSERV (electronic mailing LIST SERVer) - A program that maintains lists of electronic mail addresses. A user can request that LISTSERV add their e-mail address to a list or delete their e-mail address.

Local Area Network (LAN) - A computer network technology designed to connect computers across a short distance.

Login - The process of entering an account identifier and password to obtain access to a timesharing computer.

Lurkers - Not a derogatory term. People who merely read discussions online without contributing to them.

Kerning - Altering the horizontal space between a pair of characters to give a uniform appearance.

Kilobyte - One kilobyte is 1024 bytes (2 to the 10th power). "Kilo" is a binary analog to the decimal unit "thousand". The size of memory in a microcomputer is measured in kilobytes (Example: 256K, 512K, 640K and 1024K).

Landscape Orientation - The position of the page in which the long edge of the page runs horizontally.

Leading (Pronounced "ledding") - The amount of white space vertically between lines of type.

List Box - A box that displays a list of choices. When a list is too long to display all choices, it will have a scroll bar, so that you can view additional items.

Macro - A stored list of two or more application program commands that, when retrieved, replays the commands to accomplish a task.

Mailbox - A storage area, usually on disk, that holds incoming e-mail messages until a user reads the mail. Each mailbox has a unique address; a user must have a mailbox to receive electronic mail.

Mailing List - An electronic mail address that includes a list of recipients. Mailing lists have become popular as a way to disseminate information.

Appendix A

Menu - A list of items from which a user can select. Some Internet services permit a user to browse information by following a sequence of menus.

Menu Bar - The area at the top of an open window program containing headings for pull-down menu items.

Message Box - A type of dialog box that appears with information, a warning, an error message or a request for confirmation to carry out a command.

MIDI (Musical Instrument Digital Interface) - A format that allows communication of musical data between devices such as computers and synthesizers.

MIME - Multipurpose Internet Mail Extensions. MIME is new Internet standard for transferring nontextual data, such as audio messages or pictures, via email.

Mnemonics - Underlined, bolded or colored letters on menu commands or dialog box options indicating keystroke access for that item or option.

Modem - A device that transmits digital computer data over telephone lines. The path can consist of a long wire or a connection through the dial-up telephone system. Modems can be external or internal (built into the computer).

Mouse Button - The part of the mouse that can be "clicked" manually and that controls certain functions that may be customized to suit the user.

Mouse Pointer - A symbol that indicates a position on the screen as you move the mouse on your desk.

Multimedia - A term describing any facility that can display text, graphics, images, and sound. A computer needs special hardware to handle multimedia output.

Multi-sync Monitor - A video display monitor that is capable of automatically adjusting to the synchronization frequency of the video board that is sending signals to it.

Nanosecond - The speed of logic and memory chips is measured in nanoseconds (one billionth of a second). The RAM chips in your computer are rated in nanoseconds according to their speed. They may be 150ns, 120ns, 100ns, or 80ns chips (Electricity travels approximately one foot per nanosecond).

NetBIOS - Network Basic Input/Output System. NetBIOS is a very basic applications interface to allow an application to communicate on a network.

Netiquette - A list of suggestions for how to behave when using the Internet. Many are common sense.

NetWare - The most popular of PC local area networks by Novell, Inc. Rather than using TCP/IP as its "standard" protocol for intercomputer communications, it uses IPX/SPX. It is sometimes difficult to get a PC to "talk" TCP/IP and IPX/SPX at the same time.

Network - When two or more computers are linked together for the purpose of sharing information and/or peripheral devices, a network is created. A network is also a database design technique for managing a collection of related programs for loading, accessing, and controlling the information that makes up the database.

Network News - The name of the Internet bulletin board service.

Newsgroup - A single bulletin board in the network news service. A single user can subscribe to multiple newsgroups; each newsgroup contains articles related to one topic.

Noninterlaced Monitor - A computer monitor that does not employ the screen refresh technique called interlacing and is able to display high-resolution images without flickering or streaking.

Online /Offline - Actions performed when you are or are not actually connected to another computer.

OLE (Object Linking and Embedding) - A set of standards that allows you to create dynamic automatically updated links between documents and also to embed a document created by one application into a document created by another.

Palette - In computer video displays, the collection of colors that the system is capable of displaying.

Parallel Interface - An interface in which several bits of information (usually 1 byte) are transmitted simultaneously.

Parallel Printer - A printer that accepts information by way of a parallel interface.

Password - The secret code a user enters to gain access to a timesharing system or to obtain authorization for the FTP service. A computer does not display a password while the user enters it.

PKZIP or PKUNZIP - Suite of utilities from PKWARE for compressing and uncompressing DOS and Windows files. Uses the .zip extension.

Point-and-Click Interface - A style of interacting with a computer that uses a mouse instead of a keyboard. The user moves the mouse to position the cursor, and presses a button on the mouse to select the item under the cursor.

Appendix A

Portrait Orientation - The position of the page in which the long edge of the page runs vertically.

Printer Driver - The software that enables a program to communicate with the printer so that the program's information can be printed.

Parameter - A variable used with a command to indicate a specific value or option (Example: startup options for a program contain parameters, or arguments, that indicate how the program will run).

Path - The "address" that tells a computer where to locate a directory or file on a disk or network. A path includes the drive, the root directory and any subdirectory names that branch from the root directory.

Peripheral Device - Any external hardware device used for input/output operations with a computer system is referred to as a peripheral device. Printers, tape drives, external modems, keyboards, plotters, scanners and digitizing tablets are all examples of peripheral devices.

Pixel (Picture Element) - A pixel is the smallest dot that can be represented on a screen or in a paint (bit map) graphic.

Point Size - Unit of measure commonly used to indicate both font size and line thickness. One point equals 1/72". 72 points = 1 inch.

Port - A connection device between a computer and another component, such as a printer or modem. (Example, a printer cable is plugged into the printer port on the computer so information can be sent to the computer).

Post - To send a message to a discussion group or list.

Protocol - The rules two or more computers must follow to exchange messages. A protocol describes both the format of messages that can be sent as well as the way a computer should respond to each message.

Pull-down Menu - A pull-down menu is a window menu on the display screen that appears to be pulled downward or expanded when an item is selected from a line-bar menu. Menu items can be selected either with a mouse or with a combination of keystrokes.

RAM (Random Access Memory) - The working space or temporary storage area for the program you are using and the document on your screen. RAM is erased when the power is turned off.

ROM (Read Only Memory) - The part of a computer's main memory that contains the basic programs that run the computer when it is turned on. ROM cannot be erased.

Root Directory - The root directory is the base level of the directory structure. Branching from the root are various subdirectories, each of which can contain one or more files and/or sub directories of its own. Individual files can also reside at the root directory level. With DOS, the root directory of every disk drive is identified with the backslash character "\" and is the main directory on that drive. (Example: C:\ represents the root directory of drive C:). At the DOS prompt, to change your current directory to the root directory of drive D:, type CD\.

Route - In general, a route is the path that network traffic takes from its source to its destination. In a TCP/IP Internet, each IP datagram follows a path through a sequence of networks and routers.

Scaleable Font - A font that can be printed in virtually any point size depending on the limits of the software and printer used.

Scroll - To move the cursor through a document or list that extends beyond the screen display.

Scroll Bar - The bars on the right side and bottom of the window that let you move vertically and horizontally through a document, list or graphic by clicking on the scroll arrows or dragging the scroll box.

Server - A program that offers a service. Many computers on the Internet run servers to offer services. A user invokes a client program on their computer; the client contacts a server on a remote computer.

Sizing Handle - The small solid squares that appear on the borders of a graphics box or a graphics line that has been selected. You can drag these handles to size the box and its contents.

SMTP - Simple Mail Transport Protocol. The protocol used on the Internet to transfer mail. Eudora uses SMTP to send mail.

Source Address - The address of the computer sending data. Each packet contains the address of the source computer as well as the address of the destination computer.

Subdirectory - A subdirectory is an area on a disk for storing files. Subdirectories consist of files and/or other subdirectories. A subdirectory listing will show the names of files and subdirectories subordinate to that subdirectory along with file sizes, creation dates and times.

Surfing the Internet - A slang phrase that means, "using Internet services to browse information."

Appendix A

Syntax - The rules for organizing elements in an operation (Example: macro commands require a specific syntax or organization for them to function properly).

TELNET - The Internet remote login service. TELNET allows a user at one site to interact with a remote timesharing system at another site as if the user's terminal connected directly to the remote machine.

Terminal - A piece of hardware that lets you interact with a character based operating system such as UNIX.

Text File - A file saved in ASCII file format. It contains text, spaces and returns, but no formatting codes.

Tile - A display format for open windows. Tilled windows are displayed side by side with no window overlapping any other window.

UNIX - An extremely popular operating system in wide use on computers on the Internet. Other operating systems work fine on the Internet, but UNIX is the most common.

Upload - To send a file to another machine.

USENET - The term that applies to the group of computers that exchange network news. Some USENET sites exchange information over the Internet; others use telephone connections.

Uudecode - A UNIX program for decoding files in the uuencode format, turning them from ASCII back into binary files.

Veronica - An automated search service available through gopher. Veronica permits one to search through gopher menus for a given string. Because veronica has been integrated with gopher, one can use gopher to access veronica and to display the results of a search.

WAIS - Wide Area Information Servers. A set of full-text databases containing information on hundreds of topics. You can search WAIS using natural language queries and use relevance feedback to refine your search.

Wide Area Network (WAN) - Any network technology that can span large geographic distances.

Window - A method of displaying a document so that many of its elements appear graphically and many features are immediately available as on-screen choices. The place where you type your document is called a document window.

World Wide Web (WWW) - An Internet service that organizes information using hypermedia. Each document can contain embedded references to images, audio, or other documents. A user browses for information by following references.

WYSIWYG (What You See is What you Get) - Refers to a computer screen display that shows exactly the printed page showing fonts and graphics in correct proportions.

Write-Protect - A write-protect feature prevents a disk or tape from being written, to thereby protect any existing data. On 3.5" diskettes, the write-protect notch is a square hole punched through the shell with a slug of plastic built into the shell that can be slid over or away from the hole. When the notch or hole is closed, new data can be written to the diskette.

Zoom - To expand or reduce the image of a document or graphic on the screen. Zooming does not change the actual size of the text or graphics.

Appendix B

Popular Newsgroups

Popular Usenet Newsgroups

alt.activism
alt.computer.consultants
alt.gopher
alt.internet.services
alt.irc
biz.jobs.offered
comp.ai
comp.binaries.ibm.pc
comp.dcom.modems
comp.graphics
comp.lang.c
comp.lang.c++
comp.risks|
comp.sys.mac.hardware
comp.unix.questions
comp.windows.x
misc.education
misc.entrepreneurs
misc.forsale
misc.int-property
misc.invest
misc.jobs.contract
misc.jobs.misc
misc.jobs.offered
misc.wanted
news.announce.conferences
news.announce.important
news.announce.newusers
news.answers
news.groups
news.lists
news.newusers.questions
rec.arts.movies
rec.arts.movies.review
rec.games.misc
rec.humor
rec.humor.funny
rec.music.misc
rec.travel
rec.video

Popular World Wide Web Sites

Cable News Network (CNN): http://www.cnn.com
Cardiff's Movie Database: http://www.msstate.edu/Movies
CommerceNet: http://www.commerce.net
Cutting-Edge Computer Applications at MIT: http://tns-www.lcs.mit.edu/tns-www-home.htm
The Company Corporation: http://incorporate.com/tcc/home.html
Canadian Airlines International LTD.: http://www.CdnAir.CA
EXPO Ticket Office: http://sunsite.unc.edu/expo/ticket_office.html
FedWorld (government studies and reports etc.): http:www.fedworld.gov
Geography-What Do Maps Show?: http://info.er.usgs.gov/education/teacher/what-do-maps-show/index.html
HealthNet: http://debra.dgbt.doc.ca:80/~mike/healthnet
History and Geography: http://sunsite.unc.edu/expo/deadsea.scrolls.exhibit/intro.html
Indiana University: http://www.indiana.edu
The InterNIC Home Page (Information about the Internet): http://www.internic.net
Legal Information Institute: http://www.law.cornell.edu/lii.table.html
The Library of Congress: http://lcweb.loc.gov/homepage/lchp.html
Microsoft: http://www.microsoft.com
The Nasdaq Financial Executive Journal: http://www.law.cornell.edu/nasdaq/nasdtoc.ht
Pao Alto Medical Foundation: http://www.service.com/PAMF/home.html
Patch American High School: http://192.253.114.31/Home.html
Smiles & Emoticons: gopher://dunx1.ocs.drexel.edu/00/mail/Emoticons
Internet Shopping Mall: http://shop.internet.net
NASA:http://hypatia.gsfc.nasa.gov/NASA_homepage.html
Stanford University Medical Center: http://med-www.Stanford.EDU/MedCenter/welcome.html
Stock Market Quotes: http://www.secapl.com/cgi-bin/qsx
The Teacher Education Internet Server: http://curry.edschool.Virginia.EDU:80/teis/

Appendix B

Popular World Wide Web Sites

U.S. Department of Health and Human Services: http://www.os.dhhs.gov
Whole Internete Catalog: http://gnn.com/gnn/wic/index.html
U.S Taxation Info: http://inept.scubed.com:800/tax/tax.html

Popular Gopher Servers

Books on the Internet, from Project Gutenberg: gopher.micro.umn.edu (Choose "Libraries," then "Electronic Books.")
Economic Bulletin Board (University of Michigan): una.hh.lib.umich.edu
Electronic Newsstand (magazines, periodicals, journals): gopher.enews.com
EnviroLink Network Gopher: envirolink.org
Internet Network Information Center (InterNIC). Answers many Internet questions.: gopher.internic.net
Library of Congress: marvel.loc.gov
Metaverse (archives of music, video, and popular culture): metaverse.com
NASA Explorer (collection of images from NASA): explorer.arc.nasa.gov
Pacific Region Business: hoshi.cic.sfu.ca
Project Gutenberg (converts public book-lenghth works to electronic form): mrcnext.cso.uiuc.edu
Total Quality Management: deming.eng.clemson.edu
University of Minnesota (Information about Gopher): gopher.tc.umn.edu
University of New Brunswick (FAQs for UseNet groups included here): jupiter.sun.csd.unb.ca
U.S. Department of Education: gopher. ed.gov
U.S. Congress: gopher.house.gov or gopher.senate.gov
Wombat (On-line Dictionary of computer terms): wombat.doc.ic.ac.uk

Popular FTP Servers

(For easier use, many of these servers can be accessed through Gopher)

Cathouse (repository of television, movie, and music fun): cathouse.org
CICA (Center for Innovative Computing Applications). Many Windows shareware programs: ftp.cica.indiana.edu
Data General (collection of historical investment data about stocks, commodities, mutual funds etc.): dg-rtp.dg.com
Doctor Fun (main archive is in /pub/electronic-publications/Dr-Fun): sunsite.unc.edu
DOS games: ftp.uml.edu
Fedworld: ftp.fedworld.gov
Internet Network Information Center (InterNIC). Answers many Internet questions.: ftp.internic.net
Microsoft: ftp.microsoft.com
NCSA: ftp.ncsa.uiuc.edu
Online Book Initiative: obi.std.com
PRODUCT.COM (provides product information): ftp.product.com
Walnut Creek: ftp.cdrom.com
The OAK Software Repository (allows up to 400 anonymous logins at once) : oak.oakland.edu

As with the addresses provided with the NetCruiser Pocket Guide, this information is accurate at the time of publication. Due to the ever-changing world of the Internet, some sites may not be active.

Appendix C

Signature File Example

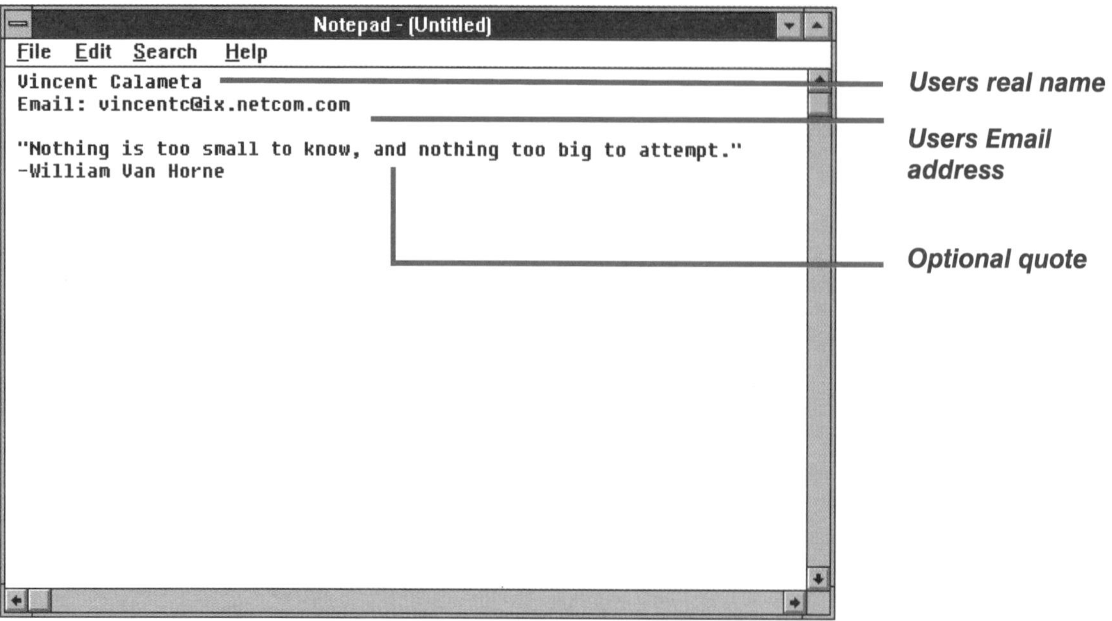

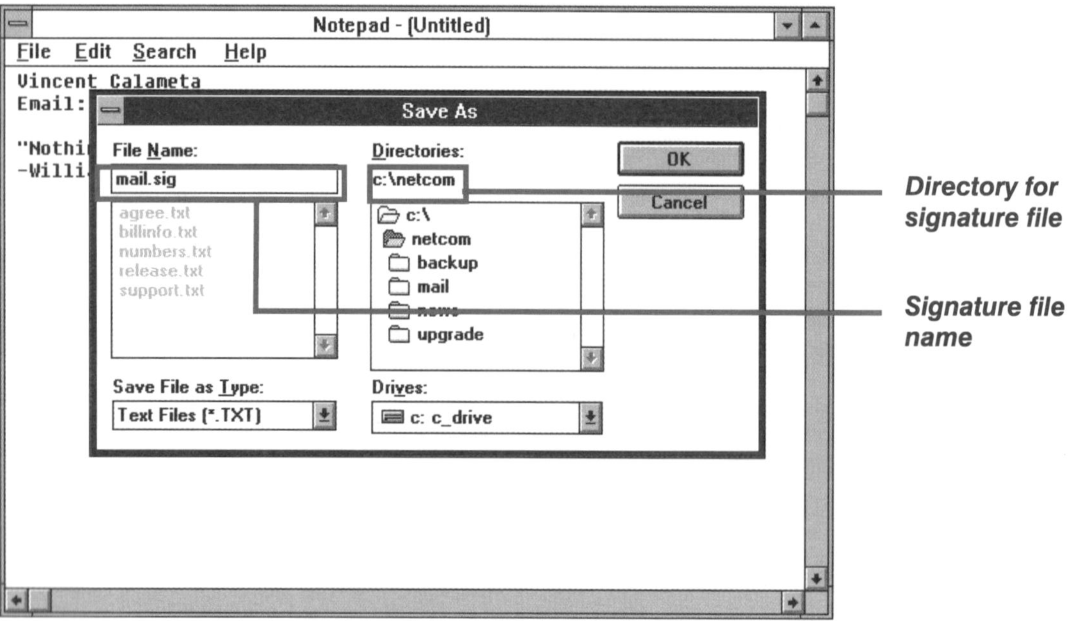

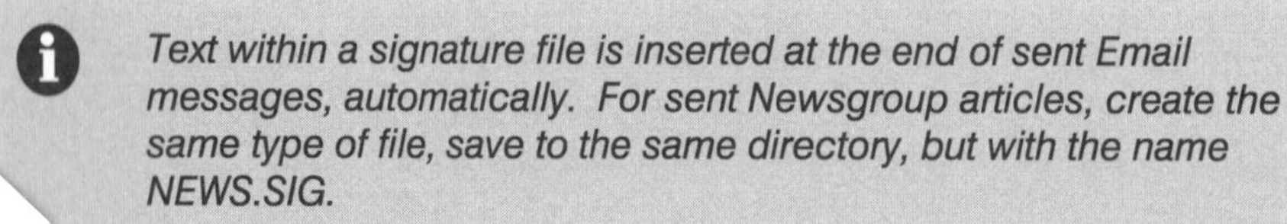

Text within a signature file is inserted at the end of sent Email messages, automatically. For sent Newsgroup articles, create the same type of file, save to the same directory, but with the name NEWS.SIG.

Other titles available from

the BEGINNER'S GUIDE Series

GUIDES

SUITES: Your Cost: $19.95

DESCRIPTION	ISBN	UPC
MS OFFICE	1-881023-87-7	7-25556-24781-4
QUICKEN HOME FINANCE	1-881023-91-5	7-25556-24796-8
MS OFFICE for Windows 95*	1-881023-94-X	7-25556-24782-1

*Titles available December 1, 1995

COMBINATIONS: Your Cost: $19.95

DESCRIPTION	ISBN	UPC
MS WINDOWS 3.1/MS DOS 5.0-6.2	1-881023-89-3	7-25556-24771-5
WordPerfect 6.1 for Windows/ 6.0 for Dos	1-881023-80-X	7-25556-24717-3

TITLES Your Cost: $19.95

DESCRIPTION	ISBN	UPC
MS WORD 6.0 for Windows	1-881023-82-6	7-25556-24727-2
MS EXCEL 5.0 for Windows	1-881023-83-4	7-25556-24752-4
MS WINDOWS 95	1-881023-90-7	7-25556-24772-2
the INTERNET	1-881023-95-8	7-25556-24792-0
MS WORD 7.0 for Windows 95*	1-881023-92-3	7-25556-24728-9
MS EXCEL 7.0 for Windows 95*	1-881023-93-1	7-25556-24753-1
MS ACCESS 7.0 for Windows 95*	1-881023-88-5	7-25556-24791-3

ToolKits

TITLES: Your Cost: $5.95

DESCRIPTION	ITEM NUMBER	UPC
MS WINDOWS 95	TKT-35772	7-25556-35772-8
LOTUS 1-2-3; Rel.5 for Windows	TKT-35707	7-25556-35707-0
WORDPERFECT 6.0 for DOS	TKT-35712	7-25556-35712-4
WORDPERFECT 6.1 for Windows	TKT-35717	7-25556-35717-9
MS WORD 6.0 for Windows	TKT-35727	7-25556-35727-8
MS EXCEL 5.0 for Windows	TKT-35752	7-25556-35752-0
MS DOS 5.0-6.2	TKT-35762	7-25556-35762-9
MS WINDOWS 3.1	TKT-35871	7-25556-35771-1
MS WINDOWS 95	TKT-35772	7-25556-35772-8
Quicken / QuickBooks	TKT-35796	7-25556-35796-4

Ordering is Easy!

By Phone: Call us at **1-800-229-2714**

Address: WizardWorks Company
3850 Annapolis Lane, Suite 100
Plymouth, MN 55447
Attn: Order Department

By Fax: Fax your order to **1-612-577-0631**
Be sure to include all your credit card info.

Ordering is Easy!

Call: 1-800-229-2714

or

Fax: 612-577-0631

or

Mail: this order form, along with your check, money order or credit card information to:

WizardWorks
3850 Annapolis Lane, Suite 100
Plymouth, MN 55447
Attn: Order Department

Please Fill Out Completely

PRODUCT NAME	QTY	PRICE	TOTAL

METHOD OF PAYMENT

☐CHECK ENCLOSED ☐MONEY ORDER ☐VISA ☐MASTERCARD

TOTAL PRODUCT	$
ADD SHIPPING & HANDLING ($4.95)	$
CANADIAN ORDERS SHIPPING & HANDLING ($6.95)	$
(MN ONLY) MN SALES TAX 6.5%	$
TOTAL ORDER	$

CARD NUMBER ____________________ EXP.DATE ________

AUTHORIZED SIGNATURE

SHIP TO:

NAME ________________________________

ADDRESS ________________________________

CITY/STATE/ZIP ________________________________

TIME TELEPHONE (___) ______________ EVENING TELEPHONE (___) ______________

Customer Satisfaction

ot fully satisfied with your WizardWorks' product, you may return it for a full refund. The product urned within 30 days of purchase with all materials including documentation, package and original sales receipt.